Sprawl and Suburbia

T0345908

HARVARD DESIGN MAGAZINE READERS
William S. Saunders, Editor

Sprawl and Suburbia

A Harvard Design Magazine Reader

Introduction by Robert Fishman

William S. Saunders, Editor

University of Minnesota Press I Minneapolis I London

These essays were previously published in *Harvard Design Magazine*, Harvard University Graduate School of Design; Peter G. Rowe, Dean, 1992–2004; Alan Altshuler, Dean, 2005–.

Thanks to coordinator Meghan Ryan for her work on *Harvard Design Magazine*.

Published by the University of Minnesota Press
111 Third Avenue South, Suite 290
Minneapolis, MN 55401-2520
http://www.upress.umn.edu

Library of Congress Cataloging-in-Publication Data

   Sprawl and suburbia : a Harvard Design Magazine reader / introduction by Robert Fishman ; William S. Saunders, editor.
      p.   cm. — (Harvard Design Magazine readers ; 2)
   Includes bibliographical references.
   ISBN 0-8166-4754-2 (hc : alk. paper) — ISBN 0-8166-4755-0 (pb : alk. paper)
   1. Suburbs—United States. 2. Land use—United States. 3. Dwellings—United States—Design and construction. 4. Suburban life—United States. I. Saunders, William S. II. Series.
   HT352.U6S67 2005
   307.76'0973—dc22

                           2005023817

Printed in the United States of America on acid-free paper

The University of Minnesota is an equal-opportunity educator and employer.

12 11 10 09 08 07 06 05   10 9 8 7 6 5 4 3 2 1

Contents

Preface
Will Sprawl Produce Its Own Demise?
William S. Saunders

"Sprawl"—the uncontrolled expansion of low-density, single-use sub-urban development into the countryside—presents itself as *the* single most significant and urgent issue in American land use around the turn of the century. Just as the word *sprawl* has entered common parlance, so too efforts to limit and reform this kind of development have become commonplace nationwide. Smart Growth and New Urbanism and belief that higher-density mixed-use nodes will decrease the need for long commutes now form the default position of most architects and urban planners, if not most urban officials. Yet sprawl is still overwhelmingly the form of new American development.

Despite the fact that many cities have seen a renaissance of their downtowns (even "non places" like downtown Los Angeles and San Diego are rapidly creating new residences, restaurants and stores, 24/7 street life, and cultural facilities), many, many more people are moving farther out to the exurbs than are moving in to the now more vibrant and safe core. And those exurbs are still almost entirely made up of tract residential houses—bigger and bigger houses—that force their owners to drive one of their three or more cars in order to do anything outside their homes. The benefits of a home with a lot of space and privacy still count for more than the benefits of being able to walk to buy bread and see a movie, and are still not offset by the detriments of long drives, social isolation, and lack of stimulation from little but the TV, the Internet, and the telephone.

Yet the tides have shifted to some small extent. And the downsides of living in sprawl will only increase as land farther and farther from urban centers is consumed and roads become more clogged. It seems inevitable that the percentage of moves *in* will grow in the coming decades.

Boredom and isolation are by no means the only reasons that reurbanization will have to increase. The age of cheap and abundant oil will be winding down in the next twenty years or so. As driving becomes more expensive, pressures will increase for a landscape of many well-distributed nodes offering the necessities of workplace, shopping, and services; it seems at least as likely that suburbs will urbanize as that city centers will densify. And looming literally as a dark cloud over this century is the now certain coming of greenhouse gas–induced climate change, which, even if reduced by the global community with green technologies, will inflict economic hardships in developed countries—and attendant limitations on mobility—unknown since the Great Depression.

The essays in this book, taken from eight years of *Harvard Design Magazine*, present, for the most part, a detailed diagnosis and analysis of the physical and social realities of sprawl at the turn of the century. Implicit and explicit is an appeal to architects, landscape architects, and urban planners and designers to move beyond their almost total preoccupation with special and singular constructions to work for the improvement of the general conditions of sprawl, of average and normative building. What these writers offer as an alternative is some form of fresh urbanism—appealing and persuasive models of life at greater density, with greater diversity, and with need-fulfilling local options.

Still, one may be skeptical that the lures of better design and lifestyle could reverse the currents of American land use. More likely it will be nasty economic and environmental pressures that force our nation's stubborn individualists to create the kind of legal structures that Alex Krieger sees as central to real change: "impact fees, user assessments, regional tax-sharing, higher gasoline taxes and highway tolls, streamlined permitting and up-zoning in already developed areas, ceilings on mortgage deductions, surcharges on second homes, open space (and related) amenity assessments, regional transfer-of-development rights, and similar ideas that may shift some of the costs of sprawl onto the sprawlers."

Sprawl's costs are already affecting sprawlers—in lost time, gasoline, rising property taxes to pay for sewer, water, and power extensions ever farther from city centers. As my barber complains that it cost him $89 to fill his SUV's gas tank, my hope for change rouses.

Introduction
Beyond Sprawl
Robert Fishman

> *A city cannot be a work of art.*
> —Jane Jacobs, The Death and Life of Great
> American Cities *(1961; italics in original)*

Jane Jacobs's admonition—*"A city cannot be a work of art"*—applies with special force to urban designers' attempts to re-form the radically innovative low-density city we persist in calling "suburbs" or "sprawl." Jacobs was not condoning ugliness; rather, her concern was that designers fail to comprehend what she calls the "complex systems of functional order" that are the true glory of cities; they mistakenly see only chaos and therefore attempt to impose a simplistic visual order that undermines the "close-grained diversity" on which cities depend. We have already learned her lesson with regard to the pedestrian-scaled districts of older cities; indeed, designers have had thousands of years of experience in devising forms that complement and intensify traditional urban complexity. The new city that has taken shape at the periphery of the old represents a much more difficult challenge. Its decentralized form and unprecedented building types constitute a radical challenge to all previous principles of urbanism. Sprawl, the pejorative but inescapable term for the low-density fragmented *city* that has become our culture's characteristic form of urbanism, is in fact a revolutionary system of urban complexity and order without traditional urban concentration.

"The city that achieves speed," Le Corbusier observed, "achieves success."[1] Since ancient times, cities achieved speed of exchange and interaction through what Spiro Kostof called "energized crowding":[2] the clustering of skills and population at a single strategic point within a region to overcome rural isolation and promote face-to-face communication.

But as the early-twentieth-century regionalists understood, innovations in transportation and communication had now made possible what Lewis Mumford called "urbanization at any point in a region."[3] One could achieve speed not by concentrating but by *fragmenting* the urban, opening up the dense fabric to allow the automobile to run free, exploding the city in fragments over whole regions. With urban functions no longer confined within the dense environment of the central city, homes, factories, offices, and stores could spread out and merge with the landscape. Here potentially was a new synthesis of speed and space unknown to urban history.

It is hardly surprising that this "transvaluation of urban values" was accomplished by professions that had little commitment to or even knowledge of the old city. Its Baron Haussmanns have been the highway engineers monomaniacally pursuing their goals of total automobility. Its Frederick Law Olmsteds have been the mortgage bankers of the Federal Housing Administration, whose guidelines for mortgage insurance have been the true arbiters of residential form. Its Daniel Burnhams have been the shopping center and office park developers who relentlessly fragmented the downtown cores—once the pride of American urbanism—to build on scattered sites at the edge of the region.

Yet this group of bureaucrats and Babbitts has, as collective regional designers, been far more revolutionary in the replacement of traditional urban form than any purported architectural avant-garde. For sprawl is a counter-modernism that takes up all the themes of the avant-garde—regional scale, speed, mass production and distribution, the merger of city and countryside—to its own ends. While architectural theorists deployed the language of deconstruction, the Babbitts have in fact deconstructed the fundamental urban binary—city and country—to produce an urban region without a dominant center or recognizable edge. Le Corbusier's Radiant City with its touching devotion to the idea of a center was a moderate compromise compared to the radical deconstruction that has in fact transformed the American metropolitan region.

Thus, the "complex systems of functional order" that underlie the sprawlscape not only are extremely powerful in themselves but also call into question all previous urban design. The region is turned inside out as the "suburbs" in almost every American region now boast the majority of population, industrial production, retail sales, and office employment. Almost every urban function that once required density and centrality now thrives in the fragmented environment of the low-density city. As the shopping center, office park, and industrial park developers soon realized, the key to location in the emerging metropolitan region was not centrality but *access*. In the freeway world, a cornfield at the edge of the region might have better access for employees and customers than a downtown "100% corner." One might say that "the suburbs" have learned to provide the full range of urbanity—except for the urban experience itself. Here too traditional forms are turned inside out. In the traditional city, crowding was ubiquitous and oppressive, and the best efforts of design turned to sculpting open space from the dense urban fabric. In the new fragmented city, it is openness that is ubiquitous and oppressive, and density becomes the goal to be patiently nurtured.

Unable to comprehend the logic of decentralization, academic critics in compensation tend to invoke a rhetoric of blanket abuse. Even now, the truly powerful critique of this system of decentralization and fragmentation comes not from the academy but from those within the system forced to acknowledge its limitations and contradictions that have become more evident as our metropolitan regions have been built out. Behind today's bureaucratic jargon and commercial boosterism, one can discern increasing unease and frustration from the very masters of sprawl. The highway engineers have largely accepted Anthony Downs's "law" that more roads inevitably mean more congestion.[4] The home builders, responsive as always to the changing market, have become increasingly restive under the single-family detached zoning they once sponsored. The once dominant regional mall has been under siege simultaneously from discount big-box "power centers" or "category killers" and from ubiquitous strip malls. And the older urban cores have, after the near-death experience of the urban crisis, seen a surprising resurrection, not least among the young and hip, whose tastes rule the future.

Most important, sprawl is now losing the support of the citizens of suburbia who have been its prime movers and beneficiaries. With only marginal leadership from planners and ecologists, the "no-growth movement" now increasingly dominates the politics of suburbia. In part, this can be explained, in Alex Krieger's words in this volume, as "some variation of 'don't harm my lifestyle by replicating the locational decisions I made a few years earlier.'" But the surprising fervor of "no growth" leads inevitably to more fundamental questioning. As I write, a seemingly routine proposal in a suburb near my home to add another strip mall to an arterial highway already pestered with them generated so large a crowd of angry citizens that the zoning hearing had to be transferred from city hall to the main auditorium of the local high school, where the crowd overflowed into the corridors. The Brookings Institution has noted more than a hundred growth-management initiatives in the most recent election cycle, over 80 percent of which passed.[5]

In short, the moment has arrived when design might achieve some critical influence over the sprawl environment: that landscape, in Ellen Dunham-Jones's words here, "almost entirely uninformed by the critical agendas or ideas" of the architectural profession and yet which "accounts for approximately 75 percent of all new construction in recent decades." But if this 75 percent is to become "the next big architectural project," as she urges (and what exactly was the last big architectural project?), then architects and planners will have to take a great leap forward: first, in their comprehension of the functional order of sprawl; second, in their ability to work productively with the multitude of private and public interests that shape the sprawl environment; and third, in their ability to creatively rethink the heritage of urban design to meet the needs of the new city. The contributors to this volume aptly express both the strengths and limitations of design at this crucial moment.

If there is a single theme that underlies all the chapters, it is the recognition that any true alternative to sprawl would not be a "style"—whether Modernist or anti-Modernist—but a profound transformation in the whole system that created the sprawl environment. Although David Harvey positions himself as a critic of the other contributors, he in fact speaks with and for them when he calls for a "utopianism of process" rather than a "utopianism of spatial form." That is, the goal is not some predetermined "right" form or density but a process that overcomes the social and physical fragmentation of sprawl itself.

One great advantage that the sprawl builders had in the past was that the very fragmentation of the environment they favored meant they could act "unilaterally," to use Andrew Ross's term here, unconstrained by the need to coordinate with others. The highway engineers gave no thought to what would be built at the end of their off-ramps, the subdividers took no responsibility for those outside their preferred income niches, and no one worried about larger impacts to the rural hinterland or the older cities. By contrast, the alternative to sprawl requires precisely that capacity for coordinated actions and alliances at the regional scale that our present economic and political system makes almost impossible. Matthew Kiefer asserts in his essay that "the popular will" in the form of "consumer preference" will be the "self-correcting mechanism" that will transform sprawl, but this market optimism underestimates the structural barriers to significant innovation. Thus it is with praise rather than criticism that I observe that most of the authors in this volume seem far more deeply engaged by the prospects for political and social change than they are by innovations in design per se.

Although all the authors aim at a synthetic view of the hoped-for transformations, I would divide the chapters into three groups according to their relative emphases. The first group emphasizes regional land use and transportation; the second, social justice; and the third, the cultural critique of suburbia.

One of the most interesting "dialogues" in this collection is between Peter Hall and Ellen Dunham-Jones. Hall's critique of what he calls "retro urbanism" has refreshingly little to do with design. In commenting on Peter Calthorpe's "Laguna West" development near Sacramento, he clearly admires its borrowings from the early-twentieth-century Garden City movement and from California domestic architecture of that period. What he critiques instead is that the plan echoes the railroad suburb—without a railroad. Through no fault of Calthorpe's, the promised light-rail line to Sacramento was never built, and thus the crucial connection between form and transportation was lost.

Although Dunham-Jones is writing about Atlanta—the promised land of sprawl—her chapter on Smart Growth helps us to understand why such connections are so difficult. As she shows, growth management in the Atlanta region is less a "mass outbreak of altruism [spurred by] evangelical Smart Growth advocates," as Matthew Kiefer skeptically describes the phenomenon, than a hardheaded attempt by the Atlanta elite to fight the pollution and congestion that have begun to strangle the region. Yet the efforts to promote transit and limit growth at the edge can be realized only through a complicated set of new regional agencies whose combination of maximum complexity and minimal funding ensures that little is actually accomplished. Her point is not that we should abandon Smart Growth but that we should understand the painfully slow and fragile alliances through which it must operate.

The subject of David Harvey's chapter is ostensibly what he calls "the communitarian trap" that lies concealed within New Urbanism. Harvey has some difficulty persuading the reader that a serious danger facing suburbia is an excess of neighborliness caused by neo-traditional design. Far more important, in my reading, is Harvey's understanding, which comes out of his research in urban social movements, that the goals of such movements (often unachieved) are less important than the sense of empowerment and community they create.[6] Middle-class suburbanites might seem sufficiently empowered already, but even they feel isolated by the rapid mutations of suburban form. Harvey's "utopianism of process" points toward an open-ended practice of urban design that emphasizes dialogue and participation over ready-made solutions.

Mike Davis has a taste for the catastrophic, and in what he elsewhere suggests will be a brief interval before the total environmental collapse of Southern California, he calls our attention to some signs of inner-city-style abandonment in the "Ozzie and Harriet" first-ring suburbs of Los Angeles like Pomona. The issue is a real one, but even Davis acknowledges it has a more positive aspect: these suburbs have become an affordable first step for many black and Latino households leaving the central city. Again, the regional context is crucial. The "at risk" suburbs could become one more victim of an unstoppable wave of abandonment, or they could be precisely where the wave stops, as affordable, diverse communities rebuild rather than degenerate.

Although Alex Krieger's consistently moderate and balanced-to-a-fault analysis of the costs and benefits of sprawl seems out of place in the context of the two fire-breathers Harvey and Davis, it is revealing that Krieger's own most trenchant critique of sprawl is the social. More usefully than Harvey or Davis, he identifies the key social issue: "The benefits of sprawl—for example, more housing for less cost with higher eventual appreciation—still tend to accrue to Americans individually, while sprawl's cost in infrastructure building, energy generation, and pollution mitigation tends to be borne by society overall." Krieger's remedies for sprawl thus swerve from design to issues of sharing the costs and benefits of sprawl equitably. Krieger's colleague Jerold S. Kayden provides a brief but incisive review of the many efforts nationwide to accomplish "diversity by law" through mandated affordable housing.

The third group of chapters puts suburbia and sprawl in the larger context of American culture today. Both Mitchell Schwarzer and James S. Russell are at their best when integrating issues specific to suburban design with larger phenomena like "spectacle" and "privatism." Schwarzer usefully relates the much derided McMansion to a society where the material world itself seems oversized; suburbia for him is precisely the intersection of the spatial freedom derived from decentralization with the consumerist demand for more of everything. But he is even more concerned that architecture itself has been overtaken and marginalized by the "society of the spectacle." He laments that "new buildings are efficient and flexible, taciturn and interchangeable," mere "backdrop for the showtime of programmed distraction."

James Russell acknowledges that the historian Sam Bass Warner traced the "privatized lives" of Americans back to our colonial origins;[7] Lewis Mumford observed that even the earliest nineteenth-century suburbs were a "collective effort to live a private life."[8] Nevertheless, there is good reason to accept his judgment that the disjunction between the ethos of privatism and the needs of American society has reached its breaking point in contemporary suburbia. Indeed, sprawl itself can be seen as the physical embodiment of privatism, and Russell demonstrates in very effective detail the truth of Alex Krieger's observation that the sprawl system represents a compulsive effort to shift costs to someone else. Russell's belief is that the search for "someone else" has finally circled back to ourselves. As suburbs are increasingly forced to bear the burdens of growth and change, a bankrupt privatism must confront a wider social vision.

Andrew Ross argues for a strong connection between the sense of security and entitlement that underlies upper-middle-class suburbia and America's post-9/11 stance of a belligerent unilateralism abroad. A historian might recall here that Truman and Eisenhower, the two presidents who presided over the golden age of suburbanization, were also both dedicated coalitionists in their foreign policies. Nevertheless, one must acknowledge the force of his question—"Why should the rest of the world be held hostage by the energy budget of the three-car American suburban home?"—a question that implicates the United States itself. James Russell's sweeping conclusion—"how America builds its [sub]urban areas is *the* critical issue of the built environment at the start of the new century"—actually understates the issue. Suburbia and sprawl are ultimately about our democracy and our survival.

2004

Notes

1. Le Corbusier, *The City of To-morrow and Its Planning* (New York: Dover, 1987; translation of *Urbanisme*, 1925), 118.

2. Spiro Kostof, *The City Shaped* (Boston: Bulfinch/Little, Brown, 1991), 37.

3. Lewis Mumford, *The Culture of Cities* (New York: Harcourt, Brace, 1938), 43.

4. Anthony Downs, *Stuck in Traffic* (Washington, DC: Brookings Institution Press, 1992).

5. Rolf Pendall, Jonathan Martin, and William Fulton, *Holding the Line: Urban Containment in the United States* (Washington, DC: Center for Metropolitan Policy, The Brookings Institution, 2003).

6. David Harvey, *Spaces of Hope* (Berkeley: University of California Press, 2000).

7. Sam Bass Warner Jr., *The Private City: Philadelphia in Three Periods of Its Growth* (Philadelphia: University of Pennsylvania Press, 1968).

8. Mumford, *Culture of Cities,* 194.

1

Seventy-five Percent: The Next Big Architectural Project

Ellen Dunham-Jones

It is a well-recognized if unwelcome fact of architectural life: architects design only a small percentage of what gets built in the United States. Still, it is astonishing that in the past quarter century a vast landscape has been produced without the kind of buildings that architects consider "architecture," a landscape almost entirely uninformed by the critical agendas or ideas of the discipline. This landscape is the suburban fringe, the outer suburbs and exurbs—the landscape often called "urban sprawl." The favored venue for development associated with the postindustrial economy, this landscape accounts for approximately 75 percent of all new construction in recent decades—yet it is shunned by most architectural designers.[1] Not only does this extraordinary phenomenon represent an immense lost opportunity for the design-bereft landscape and for architects, it also reveals the ineffectiveness of architectural discourse and theory to influence either the design of the built environment or attitudes toward societal change. However, new policies intended to ameliorate the growing pains associated with ongoing suburban development are opening up new opportunities for architects to grapple with the dilemmas posed by this landscape and to produce innovative, hybrid, and potentially critical architecture.

While it should be cause for reflection, the 75 percent figure should not come as a surprise. A traveler driving to any American city will

Scanscape. Photograph by Marc Räder.

inevitably pass through a ring of recent construction. However, because so much of this new building is generic in design, if not downright ugly, and because it is spread out at low densities or hidden from
view in cul-de-sacs, this vast body of work rarely figures in discussions
of contemporary architecture. The prevalent attitude in architectural
discourse—and not without reason—is that malls, office park buildings, apartment complexes, and suburban houses are overwhelmingly
formulaic, market-driven, unimaginative designs unworthy of the designation "architecture." Despite the current fascination with 1950s
styling and the rediscovery of the California Case Study houses, the
suburbs do not represent "modern living" to the generation of designers actually raised in them. Beyond the revived chic of butterfly roofs,
boomerang curves, and texture and pattern in cladding, much recent
architecture resembles midcentury work in its rejection of place-based
forms in favor of more Modernist expressions of an international or
global style.[2] But architects tend to dismiss the suburbs as culturally
vapid, still bound by the stubbornly patriarchal conventions of Ozzie
and Harriet.[3] Those who value the potential of architecture to challenge the status quo feel particularly alienated by suburbia's apparent

complacency, especially its 1950s-cum-1990s belief in the American way, its abundant consumption, trust in authority, and the communal conformity that often masks the inequities of a system that literally zones out difference.

A few of us teaching design have enjoyed exploring this *terrain vague* in studios in which the banality of the 'burbs takes on a kind of B-movie hipness. A class trip to Wal-Mart or Home Depot is a walk on the wild side for the intrepid men and women dressed in black. But by and large, our discipline has ignored the entire landscape that contains the bulk of new building.[4] The schools teach ways to think about cities and the natural landscape but present few paradigms for working with the murky conditions in between. The architectural profession, with a few notable exceptions, remains focused on the design of single buildings with little concern about where they are located.[5] Many design journals have reported on New Urbanism with varying degrees of skepticism, but they have generally shown little interest in the suburbs or suburban building types. With blithe inconsistency, architects and architectural scholars point to the seemingly undesigned sprawl of suburbia and say, "Don't blame us, we had nothing to do with it." This avoidance is precisely the problem.

It is no small matter for architects to write off suburban and ex-urban buildings as "not our concern." In fact, their contribution to this landscape is more significant than is generally acknowledged. Certainly, many suburban building types rely heavily on cookie-cutter reproduction with little input from architects; this is especially true in the case of single-family houses. Whether built by large production home builders or small contractors, suburban house designs are more and more alike, as increasingly well-distributed and sophisticated marketing information steers builders toward variations on the same few plans.[6] Stand-alone retail franchises, hotels, and storage facilities similarly rely on standardized templates, especially if they belong to one of the ever-expanding national chains.[7] However, architects are very much involved in designing the building types that are allowing the continued expansion of peripheral development and dramatically changing the contemporary suburbs: office and commercial space, shopping areas, suburban multifamily housing, and schools and other public or institutional buildings.[8] And yet architects' work on these projects is rarely acknowledged—either for its intelligence or lack thereof. While sylvan corporate campuses, aggressive attention-seeking retail, and high-end institutional projects get published with some frequency, they are almost never described as "suburban," whereas the "urbanity" of city buildings is often celebrated. To most architects today, "urban" implies a degree of vitality and innovation not associated with the assumed conventionality and middlebrow tastes of the suburbs. This blinkered view is relatively new. In the first half of the twentieth century, architects and critics from Frank Lloyd Wright to the founders of CIAM to Lewis Mumford recognized the value of considering architecture in relation to the full range of contexts that connect the city and its suburbs to the larger region.[9] Contemporary discussions of buildings more often present them in terms of professional or theoretical discourse rather than in terms of their participation in a specific urban or regional context.[10] As a consequence, the profession has more or less abdicated responsibility for its role in designing contemporary suburbia.

This bias against suburbia disengages architects from the environment in which half of Americans now live and work.[11] Not only does this disengagement reinforce the common perception of architects as elitist, it also guarantees the marginalization of the profession. Is it a coincidence that while the suburbs were experiencing tremendous expansion, architectural discourse shifted from the 1950s and 1960s focus on practice to the 1970s and 1980s focus on theory? Perhaps this can be explained by the degree to which suburban developers have valued the predictable market performance of conventional designs more than architectural innovation. The limitations of working for developers and their largely conservative middle-class clients enhanced the appeal of operating in more hypothetical and intellectual realms. Theory-oriented designers claimed the high road as they declared their autonomy from context and commerce, staking positions from which to critique the wider culture. Architectural theorists, in particular, have become increasingly isolated from both practice and the dominant landscape of everyday life.

Meanwhile the high road has failed to provide the professional autonomy it seemed to promise: Elite clients interested in distinguishing themselves from middle-class conventions soon discovered that the unconventional projects of the neo-avant-garde suited them much like designer-label fashion. Today, despite growing attention to new technologies, urban design, and environmental and energy agendas, it is not theory or critique that dominates architectural discourse so much as agenda-less celebrity. The signature styles of star designers are sought on increasingly predictable and limited short lists for major cultural institutions worldwide. Such recognition of the value of distinctive design deserves to be celebrated. Sadly, however, it also perpetuates the sense that architecture is a clubby profession principally concerned with serving the wealthy, a profession cut off from everyday life and indifferent to the larger influence it might enjoy.

The same critique has also often been applied to Washington ("Beltway") politicians, but they have been quicker to recognize how power and population have shifted toward the suburbs.[12] The fact is that suburbia no longer conforms to the now outdated postwar stereotypes that earned it the disdain of so many architects.[13] Suburbs today incorporate conditions as varied as the glittering office buildings of edge cities and the multiethnic mini-malls of older first-ring suburbs. While many suburbs are struggling with out-of-control growth, others are struggling with disinvestment. While some are still bedroom communities, many have become the engines of the New Economy, more connected to global business ventures than to local development.[14] Henry L. Diamond and Patrick F. Noonan, authors of *Land Use in America*, report that approximately 95 percent of the fifteen million new office jobs created in the 1980s were in low-density suburbs.[15] Various studies in the mid-1990s of the fastest-growing businesses and

Near O'Hare Airport, Illinois, 1991. Photograph copyright Bob Thall.

areas of job growth also show them all in the suburbs.[16] And while one can still find neighborhoods populated by traditional families, in 1999 only 7 percent of U.S. households had a working dad, a stay-at-home mom, and children under eighteen.[17] Suburban households increasingly reflect the changing demographics of the country—65 percent of households do not have children, and 25 percent of households are people living alone.[18] All of which suggests that the suburbs are not as "suburban" as they used to be.

In fact, the suburbs have become the centers of innovation, the fuel cells of the New Economy. Silicon Valley is the preeminent example of a high-tech suburban landscape producing leading-edge products for a global marketplace. Simultaneously an instance of decentralization and low-density agglomeration, its example has been imitated throughout the United States by start-up businesses in search of cheap space, shared supply routes, and a highly educated workforce.[19] While much of the office stock in the suburbs continues to be filled with the back offices of the service economy and thus remains technologically tethered to central cities, the majority of businesses in recent suburban developments—from hardware and software developers to new media and biotech companies—are oriented to global rather than local markets.

And with growth have come growing pains. The suburbs have become centers of emerging social, economic, and environmental problems. Architects interested in confronting issues of mobile capital, social fragmentation, complexity, environmental justice, or sustainability will find rich grist for their mills in the suburbs. Commonly lumped together under the term *sprawl,* these dilemmas reflect the encroachment of problems once considered "urban" into the landscape of the American Dream. Suburbanites increasingly complain—with reason—about traffic congestion, road rage, rising taxes, municipal debt, crime, pollution, loss of open space, lack of affordable housing, and out-of-control development.[20] As the suburbs and urban fringe have absorbed the spaces of the New Economy, the same development standards that once promised a retreat from the city—densities below three to four dwelling units per acre, auto dependency, a road system designed to minimize traffic in residential areas, single-use zoning, discontiguous developments and stand-alone buildings—now trigger sprawl.

The tipping point between a healthy poly-nucleated region and sprawling leapfrog development is not always clear and is, in fact, the subject of much academic debate.[21] Arguments in defense of decentral-

Highway, housing, mountains. Photograph by Bill Owens.

ized development patterns tend to view them as the efficient workings of the free market, which provide an ever-higher standard of living to more and more Americans.[22] Critics, prone to invoking the pejorative "sprawl," are more likely to point to the spatial segregation of rich and poor, continued racial segregation, imbalances between jobs and housing, public services inequities, decay and disinvestment in first-ring and older suburbs, self-defeating tax incentives spurred by competing municipalities, increased land consumption per capita, increased vehicle miles traveled per capita, more impermeable surfaces, declining air and water quality, increased flooding, loss of animal habitat, and a general loss of civic engagement and social capital.[23]

Precisely because of the depth and interconnectedness of these problems, the suburbs have increasingly become centers of innovative policies and proposed solutions. Many of these are grouped together under the still nebulously defined term "Smart Growth," coined by the Environmental Protection Agency to designate policies that help cities conform to the environmental standards of the Clean Air and Clean Water Acts. While the EPA targeted smokestack and sewage pipe emissions throughout the 1970s and 1980s, 1990s-style Smart Growth combats automobile emissions and polluting runoffs produced by sprawl development patterns and land-use regulations.[24] Instead of the no-growth policies favored by many environmentalists but resisted by affordable housing advocates and free marketeers, Smart Growth encourages regional-scale planning that identifies both natural areas to be preserved and growth areas targeted for higher-density, transit-oriented development. By coordinating federal, state, and local investments in infrastructure, transit routes, and job centers, Smart Growth links economic development, land-use planning, and environmental protection.[25]

Part of the strategy of Smart Growth is to focus responsibility for the maintenance of environmental quality less on government regulations and big business practices, and more on local growth patterns and individual lifestyle choices. Municipalities are encouraged to engage in Smart Growth planning with federal funds made available through the Clinton-Gore administration's Livable Communities Initiative. A thirty-point plan, the initiative includes proposals for $10.75 billion worth of "Better America Bonds" to support local efforts to preserve open space and protect water, for $9.1 billion to promote transportation alternatives and brownfield mitigation, and for $35 million to fund local computer mapping to aid regional planning.[26] Smart Growth policy makers complement these incentives with an increasing emphasis on quality-of-life arguments that echo suburbanites' frustrations and promote the benefits of living in towns and urban neighborhoods instead of subdivisions. Harriet Tregoning, director of the Urban and Economic Development Division of the EPA and coordinator of the Smart Growth Network, points out that although 80 percent of Americans call themselves "environmentalists," few of them display this leaning in their life circumstances—beyond engaging in curbside recycling and perhaps buying the Eddie Bauer model of the SUV.[27]

Smart Growth policies are intended to spur development patterns that allow citizens to make more environmentally, socially, and economically sustainable lifestyle decisions.

While Smart Growth and Livable Communities are concerned more with regional than with architectural design, they are nonetheless enabling architects to participate more effectively in the development of the neglected 75 percent. Two professional programs, the AIA's Center for Livable Communities and the Congress for the New Urbanism, have engaged in shaping public policies through bringing together architects, planners, and high-ranking policy officials. More than fifty sessions at the 2000 AIA convention were related to Livable Communities; more are planned for coming years. New Urbanism is similarly growing. In the eight years since its founding, the Congress for the New Urbanism has grown to 2,100 members and has formed alliances with the U.S. Department of Housing and Urban Development, the EPA, Fannie Mae, the Urban Land Institute, the MacArthur Foundation, and the Energy Foundation. Because much of its development has been located in greenfield sites and has employed neo-traditional styling, New Urbanism is often dismissed as New Suburbanism. What such criticism fails to recognize is how such styling helps sell the far more radical—and urban—aspects of New Urbanist proposals, including mixed uses, mixed incomes, mixed building types, higher densities, and better public transit.[28] While few New Urbanist developments have been adequately linked to larger regional growth plans, in urban, suburban, and exurban sites they have offered residents alternatives to conventional sprawl.

While many architects continue to view New Urbanists with suspicion, the movers and shakers of the New Economy are increasingly recognizing the benefits of its principles. In what might be a telling irony, Silicon Valley has decided that rather than relying on telecommuting and e-commerce to relieve its congested roads and long commutes, it should invest in public transit and affordable housing. The Silicon Valley Manufacturing Group—representing all the major Silicon Valley employers in coalition with the twenty-one municipalities in Santa Clara County—pushed for and won a ½¢ sales tax to fund $2.5 billion in roads and rail and to build 24,000 affordable houses.[29] In Portland, Oregon, all Intel workplaces are now within ten minutes of a light-rail station or bus stop, and the company provides all 11,000 employees with a transit pass. In Atlanta, BellSouth is consolidating its 13,000 employees, now located in seventy-five suburban locations, into three new locations close to transit stations in the center of the city. In addition, BellSouth is constructing additional parking decks with small business centers at four suburban transit stops so that employees can begin, conclude, or even conduct their workdays there, thus offering them the chance to avoid rush-hour commutes.

Similarly, many designers of digital networks are beginning to recognize the value to their employees of face-to-face interactions and of ecologically sound and socially diverse environments. Microsoft has hired Peter Calthorpe to relocate its corporate campus and integrate it into an urban neighborhood. The plan calls for office buildings to line streets adjacent to the walkable, transit-served, mixed-use town center of Issaquah Highlands; restaurants and a health club that once would have been internally situated will instead be placed in the town center, near shops and residences. Employers in many businesses, but especially those in high-tech, are finding that in a highly competitive labor market they need to offer more amenities to attract and retain employees. This is not simply a matter of fancy gyms and cafeterias. Especially when job tenures are short and industries are competitive, prospective employees evaluate the overall quality of life in a region. Instead of a boxy building in the middle of a large lot in the middle of endless sprawl, employees who can afford to be selective are looking for access to sociable, walkable, mixed-use neighborhoods and to hiking trails, beaches, and parks. A recent study showed that high-tech firms ranked overall environmental quality as a top factor in location decisions, one that helps them attract talented employees.[30] A similar study also noted the preference among the rising generation for culturally and demographically diverse populations.[31]

These findings support the dissatisfaction of New Economy leaders with the kind of sterile suburban environments in which so many of them have been working. The new dot.coms are discovering that Silicon Valley is a terribly inefficient place. With venture capital easier to obtain, emerging digital ventures are more willing to pay the higher rents of Silicon Alley in New York or Media Gulch in San Francisco, places more attractive to their employees. Such places offer lively, compact, twenty-four-hour, mixed-use environments and facilitate the networking and access to amenities that time-pressured workers prefer (they also reduce the distance-sensitive costs of providing high bandwidth computer links). The atmosphere of these urban places is much less corporate and far funkier than that of a suburban office park.

Similarly, renovated warehouses, often in gentrifying neighborhoods like San Francisco's Mission Hill and in Atlanta between Auburn Avenue and the old Fourth Ward, provide spacious, informal, and weathered settings that highlight the aggressive newness of the dot.coms. Precisely because telecommunications increasingly allow businesses to locate anywhere, this kind of recentralization is occurring more and more. In both cases, New Economy businesses are selecting certain locations less because they reduce costs than because they appear to offer a better quality of life. Thus, even in suburban settings, the New Economy is promoting better design, community, and environmental standards.

What remains is for architects to seize these opportunities. Given Smart Growth's mandates for higher densities and innovative mixed-use environments and the New Economy's market pressures for healthy, lively, 24-7 environments, there is a growing need for architects to take the skills they have honed on urban projects—the creative integration of mixed uses and complex site requirements—out to the suburbs. But they should first leave behind their prejudices about suburban life and learn to recognize the dynamics of transformation already in place. Many of the older suburbs of Los Angeles, for instance, are being adapted to new ways of life—entrepreneurial, often immigrant homeowners use their front yards as retail spaces and their carports as commercial spaces.[32] These ad hoc live-work arrangements suggest the need for greater attention to the complexities of running businesses from the home and of accommodating telecommuting.[33] Malls and retail environments are similarly looking for new formats to distinguish themselves from competitors and to meet the challenge of Internet retailing. Some suburbs are renovating older malls or building new ones to create town centers and main streets where none existed.[34] Hybrids combining libraries, post offices, shops, recreation, restaurants, and even residences, these centers are generally more innovative in their mix of programs than in their design expression or commitment to civic purposes, but they do reflect an interest in urbanizing suburbia. In such contexts, architects have extraordinary opportunities and abilities to show how innovative design can help the suburbs define their identities, generate community pride, and compete in the New Economy.

The suburban problem is not just an urban design problem—it is also an architectural problem. That suburbs can be improved through new architectural ideas is brilliantly exemplified by the work of Gary Reddick and his firm Sienna Architecture Company of Portland, Oregon. Sienna has been exploring innovative ways of melding different suburban building types to form hybrid urban buildings that nonetheless retain a suburban level of service, convenience, and name-brand recognition. By stacking housing above parking lots and retail chain stores, Sienna is providing the mixed uses and higher densities advocated by Smart Growth.[35] In Seattle and Portland, where there are very good markets for residential development, Sienna convinced a variety of nonresidential building owners to sell the air rights over their parking lots or roofs for housing. In Portland's desirable and compact Northwest neighborhood, Sienna saw the parking lot of a specialized medical center as a potential housing site. After producing a pro forma, the firm approached the owners and showed that it could provide them with a covered, forty-three-space parking lot (with only

Sienna Architecture Company, Northrup Commons, Portland, Oregon, 1997. Photograph courtesy of Sienna Architecture Company.

three fewer spaces than before) and a million-dollar profit in exchange for stacking an additional layer of parking (with a separate entry) and two stories of condominiums. The built project, Northrup Commons, screens the parking with duplexes entered from the streets and adds two floors of apartments. The resulting section weaves conventional flats, duplexes, and parking infrastructure into a unique mix whose massing, scale, and materials fit remarkably well into its traditional context.

Sienna has also pioneered the building of apartments and condominiums on top of grocery stores. Its design for Macadam Village, three miles from downtown Portland, places apartments on the roof of an upscale grocery store and retail strip. The apartments face several Sienna-designed multifamily villas built into the side of a hill. The level of the retail strip and the level of the housing are distinct, each level more or less conforming to typological expectations (including a surface parking lot in front of the retail). But these two uses are resolved into an unusually tight urbanistic whole. Back-of-house deliveries and garbage storage are tucked under the access road to the housing and present no disincentive for nearby residential development. This level of care drives up costs, as do the HVAC and roof structure—but such costs are paid for by the sale of the roof's air rights.

In downtown Portland, Sienna initiated a wave of redevelopment around the North Park Blocks by fitting residential units and structured parking neatly into a ninety-two-year-old automotive warehouse. The designers oriented the condominiums toward the park and reused the car ramps to provide three levels of parking near the interior of the block. Residents on the lower levels of the now ten-story building can park more or less in front of their units. Four new floors were added above the condominiums. Prices for the units range from $113,000 to $573,000. The diversity in the range of home prices and presumably in the income levels of the residents is underscored by how the design combines its various elements: the new, chic penthouse hat, an old painted billboard that has been left on one elevation, and a proposed restaurant at street level looking out at the park. The result is a strikingly urban juxtaposition of old and new, rich and middle-income, residential and commercial—all with internal and invisible parking.

In Seattle, Reddick and his firm have convinced Safeway to allow construction of 100 units of housing above a 65,000-square-foot store fit tightly onto its site. The sale of the roof rights will not only pay for the project's two levels of internal parking (including a full-service truck dock) but will also provide the grocery store with an in-house clientele. Using similar arguments, Sienna hopes to convince a national drugstore chain to allow construction of an assisted living complex above its roof.[36]

The landscape of America is covered by—littered with—stand-alone chain stores selling everything from groceries to medicines to books. The national chains in particular have resisted adapting their design templates to connect and coordinate with other uses and to contribute to more compact urban places. In this context, Sienna's piggybacking strategies are downright revolutionary and bode especially well for retrofitting existing suburban retail strips targeted for Smart Growth.

Big problems provide big opportunities for creative and resourceful people. Architects who look to the suburbs and engage themselves in the process of development have a tremendous opportunity to challenge the status quo and radically reimagine the suburban landscape. Mayors, governors, developers, and suburbanites desperately need alternatives to sprawl, and architects need to be reengaged practically— and theoretically—with the unavoidable issues of ecological sustainability, social justice, mobile capital, consumer culture, ethnic and cultural identities, and politics. The new models, new policies, and new demographics I have been discussing should empower architects to move beyond merely representing or critiquing these problems. This is not a call for producing new templates, replacing one suburban formula with another. Nor is it intended to detract from cities. Rather I am arguing that architects should bring their urban sensibilities to bear on the 75 percent of development that they have usually been ignoring. It is because I am an urbanist that I am arguing that greater attention be paid to the suburbs.

There are many reasons for architects to get involved with the design of suburbia. Like the New Urbanists, they might be motivated by a reformist desire to redirect and reconfigure suburban development to advance social and environmental goals. Or they might be attracted by the business opportunities offered by the New Economy. Or by the opportunity to critically engage the rapidly transforming suburban culture. There are many questions that critics, theorists, and designers might ask about this transformation. How can architecture contribute to the leading of an admirable contemporary life in suburbia? How can architecture better deal with middle-class identities and tastes? How might the increasing mass customization of products (from Levis to kitchen cabinets to entire construction systems) help decrease suburban homogeneity and spur consumer demand for better architecture and design? How might suburbia be retrofitted without replicating the dilemmas of gentrification? Seventy-five percent of the landscape and 50 percent of the population await our answers.

2000

Notes

1. Seventy-five percent is a conservative approximation based on various indices (and their less-than-consistent terms of measurement). It refers strictly to the United States. Development patterns in other nations, including Brazil, India, and Indonesia, are producing mega-cities whose populations dwarf those of U.S. metropolises. In the United States, however, population growth is concentrated in the suburban peripheries. Growth rates have varied across the country. Cushman & Wakefield, the real estate firm, reports that in 1999, 5.5 million square feet of new office space was added to American cities, while 69 million square feet, or 92.6 percent, was added to suburban markets; see Peter Grant, "Commercial Real-Estate Boom Cools," *Wall Street Journal,* June 22, 2000. That is a significant increase from the 1980s, when cities with prosperous downtowns retained 40 percent of new office space, losing only 60 percent of this market to suburbia, and weaker cities lost 80 to 85 percent of their market to their suburbs; see William C. Wheaton, "Downtowns versus Edge Cities: Spatial Competition for Jobs in the 1990s," WP45, MIT Center for Real Estate, 1993. In contrast to commercial space, housing has been more stable. Of the Census Bureau's three categories—Central Cities, Suburbs (which with Cities constitute a Metropolitan Statistical Area, or MSA), and Outside MSAs—suburbs contain the significant majority of households. In 1995, there were 97,693,000 households in the United States; 30,243,000 in cities, 45,864,000 (47 percent) in suburbs, and 21,586,000 outside metropolitan areas. Between 1993 and 1995, 82 percent of new metropolitan households and 61 percent of new households overall were in suburbia; these data come from the 1993 and 1995 Census American Housing Surveys. Similarly, in 1986, 1991, and 1998, more than 80 percent of new housing construction was in the suburbs; see Alexander von Hoffman, "Housing Heats Up: Home Building Patterns in Metropolitan Areas" (Center on Urban and Metropolitan Policy, in collaboration with the Joint Center for Housing Studies at Harvard University and the Brookings Institute, Survey Series: December 1999), 1. From 1990 to 1998, 76.2 percent of the population growth in metropolitan regions was outside the central cities; these data were obtained from the Population Estimates Program of the U.S. Census Bureau.

2. Nonetheless, there are similarities in how some current work and work

from the 1950s expressed their contemporaneity. See Hans Ibelings, *Super-modernism: Architecture in the Age of Globalization* (Rotterdam: Netherlands Architecture Institute, 1998).

3. While there are many examples, Neil Smith's recent reading of Seaside exemplifies the tendency for architecture critics to assume that neotraditional architectural styles appeal to and foster neotraditional lifestyles, such as apron-clad women in kitchens; see "Which New Urbanism? The Revanchist 90s," *Perspecta 30* (Cambridge, MA: MIT Press, 1999).

4. Notable exceptions include Peter G. Rowe's study of suburban building types and development in *Making a Middle Landscape* (Cambridge, MA: MIT Press, 1991); Rem Koolhaas's writings on Atlanta, Generic Cities, Lite Urbanism, and Bigness, in O.M.A., Rem Koolhaas, and Bruce Mau, *S,M,L,XL* (New York: Monacelli Press, 1995); and the efforts of the New Urbanists; see Michael Leccese and Kathleen McCormick, eds., *Charter of the New Urbanism* (New York: McGraw-Hill, 2000).

5. The AIA's Center for Livable Communities and the interest of many AIA chapters in local urban design issues are welcome exceptions to the AIA's dominant interests.

6. Profit margins are so slim and competition for market share so severe in the new housing market that a single proven popular house design can dominate production. Marketing analyst Laurie Volk of Zimmerman/Volk Associates estimates that in 1999, one particular design accounted for as much as 30 percent of all new single-family detached housing throughout the country.

7. Aided by digital coordination of inventory and distribution, corporate chains are increasing their share of their respective markets. Wal-Mart now accounts for more than 5 percent of all retail spending in the United States. Independent booksellers claimed 58 percent of book sales in 1972, just 17 percent in 1997. By 1998 Home Depot and Lowe's accounted for almost 25 percent of all hardware and building supply sales. Since 1986, the growth of Office Max, Office Depot, and Staples has caused small and medium-sized office products stores to lose ground: their share of this market declined from 20 percent to 4 percent. See Stacy Mitchell, *The Home Town Advantage: How to Defend Your Main Street against Chain Stores . . . And Why It Matters* (Minneapolis: Institute for Local Self-Reliance, 2000).

8. A 1985 survey of developers of multifamily housing found that half of them used in-house designers. The other building types listed are far more likely to hire outside design services. See Robert Gutman, *Architectural Practice: A Critical View* (New York: Princeton Architectural Press, 1988). Growth in these building types is reflected in the following statistics: Between 1960 and 1980, the stock of apartments in complexes with more than ten dwellings increased threefold in the San Diego SMSA, almost sevenfold in the Houston SMSA, and eightfold in the Phoenix SMSA. In the Puget Sound area they house almost 20 percent of the suburban population, more than half of the

city of Seattle. See Anne Vernez Moudon and Paul Mitchell Hess, "Suburban Clusters," *Wharton Real Estate Review* 1 (spring 1999). While central cities housed approximately 42 percent of corporate headquarters in 1984, by the early 1990s this number was down to 29 percent due to relocations to the suburbs. See U.S. Congress, Office of Technology Assessment, *The Technological Reshaping of Metropolitan America,* OTA-ETI-643 (Washington, DC: U.S. Government Printing Office, September 1995), 48. While population grew 10 percent in the 1980s, retail floor space grew 80 percent, most of it in malls or discount stores in the suburbs. See Ian F. Thomas, "Reinventing the Regional Mall," *Urban Land,* February 1994, 25.

9. In a similar manner, Andres Duany has recently developed the concept of the "rural-urban transect." Inspired by how nature distributes species along the continuum from wetlands to uplands to foothills, the transect categorizes types of locations from rural edges to urban cores, using this to relate the design of individual buildings and neighborhoods to larger contexts. See Andres Duany, Elizabeth Plater-Zyberk, and Jeff Speck, *Suburban Nation: The Rise of Sprawl and Decline of the American Dream* (New York: North Point Press, 2000); and Duany, Plater-Zyberk & Co., *The Lexicon of the New Urbanism* (Miami: Duany, Plater-Zyberk & Co., version 2.0, 1999).

10. This is particularly evident in the tendency of journals to discuss buildings in relation to a theme or to compare them to buildings of the same type. Ironically, journals aimed at developers, such as *Urban Land,* are more prone to feature articles on a particular city, although they do so to examine how market forces have affected development.

11. The 1995 Census American Housing Survey showed that 47 percent of American households were in suburbs, and that suburbs were growing at a faster rate than either cities or outside MSAs. It is reasonable to expect that the 2000 census will show that the majority of Americans live in suburbs.

12. According to the Congressional Quarterly Weekly Report of May 1997, suburban congressional districts outnumbered urban districts two to one, rural districts three to one. The significance of this is discussed by G. Scott Thomas, *The United States of Suburbia: How the Suburbs Took Control of America and What They Plan to Do with It* (Amherst, NY: Prometheus Books, 1998).

13. Robert Wilson, editor of *Preservation* magazine, recently made this point in "Enough Snickering. Suburbia Is More Complicated and Varied than We Think," *Architectural Record,* May 2000.

14. Nicholas Lemann argues this point in his study of Philadelphia's transformation from a banking center to a branch-office city whose business power base has largely shifted to the suburbs, eroding the power of the city's traditional civic elite. "Two of the most prominent and rapidly growing Philadelphia companies, for example, are Vanguard, the mutual-fund empire, and QVC, the home-shopping television network. Both serve national markets

from isolated locations in the suburbs." See "Letter from Philadelphia: No Man's Town, The Good Times Are Killing Off America's Local Elites," *The New Yorker,* June 5, 2000.

15. Henry L. Diamond and Patrick F. Noonan, eds., *Land Use in America* (Washington, DC: Lincoln Institute of Land Policy and Island Press, 1996), 94.

16. F. Kaid Benfield, Matthew D. Raimi, Donald D. T. Chen, *Once There Were Greenfields: How Urban Sprawl Is Undermining America's Environment, Economy, and Social Fabric,* Natural Resources Defense Council, Surface Transportation Policy Project (New York: NRDC Publications, 1999), 14.

17. From a presentation by Marcie Pitt-Catsouphes of the Center for Work and Family at Boston College at the conference "Is Design a Catalyst for Community?" held in Seaside, Florida, in January 2000.

18. In 1998 the Census Bureau defined 69 percent of the 102.5 million households as "family households." However, only 49 percent of those contained children under the age of eighteen. This means that 33.8 percent of households had children; data obtained from U.S. Bureau of the Census, Current Population Reports, Series P20-515, *Household and Family Characteristics: March 1998,* Update (Washington, DC: U.S. Government Printing Office, 1998). In 1996, 25 percent of households were married families with children (the conventional suburban stereotype), the same percentage of households of people living alone. See the U.S. Bureau of the Census, Current Population Reports, Series P23-194, *Population Profile of the United States: 1997* (Washington, DC: U.S. Government Printing Office, 1998), 24.

19. Christopher Leinberger has tracked the complex factors driving leapfrog development and new generations of metropolitan cores; see "Metropolitan Development Trends of the Late 1990s: Social and Environmental Implications," in Diamond and Noonan, eds., *Land Use in America.*

20. The swell of suburban discontent can be gauged by the growing willingness of voters to fund anti-sprawl initiatives. In 1998 and 1999, more than three hundred ballot measures in more than twenty-five states were approved, authorizing $9 billion to buy and conserve open space, protect farmland, and clean up brownfields. See "Building Livable Communities, A Report from the Clinton-Gore Administration," rev. June 2000 (Washington, DC: Livable Communities, 2000). See also Richard Lacayo, "The Brawl over Sprawl," *Time,* March 22, 1999; and "Sprawl: The Revolt in America's Suburbs," *New Democrat,* March/April 1999.

21. See in particular, "Alternative Views of Sprawl," a pairing of articles by Peter Gordon and Harry W. Richardson, "Are Compact Cities a Desirable Planning Goal?" and Reid Ewing, "Is Los-Angeles-Style Sprawl Desirable?" *Journal of the American Planning Association,* Winter 1997.

22. The defense-of-sprawl arguments are well summarized by Christopher R. Conte, "The Boys of Sprawl," *Governing,* May 2000.

23. Among the many critiques of sprawl are *Once There Were Greenfields*

and *Suburban Nation*, both cited above. I have also discussed this topic in "Temporary Contracts: The Economy of the Post-Industrial Landscape," *Harvard Design Magazine*, Fall 1997.

24. The shift in focus is due partly to the EPA's relative success at reducing industrial pollution and partly to widespread recognition of the exponential damage that could be caused by sprawl were projected population increases to be accommodated by current development patterns. In a January 13, 2000, press release, the Census Bureau projects that the U.S. population will grow from 273 million to 404 million (a 50 percent increase) by 2050 and will more than double by 2100.

25. Both Smart Growth and Livable Communities have been criticized as pandering to suburban voters by promising to preserve their current lifestyles while not allowing others to enjoy these lifestyles. Intended to sponsor both infill into existing communities and more responsible and directed growth, rather than no growth, both policies are nonetheless subject to abuse in local politics.

26. See "Building Livable Communities," cited above.

27. Tregoning also notes that one of the accomplishments of Smart Growth has been to encourage EPA's core supporters—the committed environmentalists and Sierra Club members, for instance—to shift from resisting growth of any kind toward accepting the social and economic benefits of growth that is strategic and environmentally friendly; from a conference presentation on "Building and Rebuilding Suburban Neighborhoods," December 1999, the Seaside Institute, Seaside, Florida.

28. New Urbanists are still contentious about the subject of style. Marketing aside, some of us feel strongly that traditional styles best connect to the history and climate of places. Others of us are anxious to demonstrate how modern designs can fit into both time and place and feel frustrated that American home buyers and mortgage lenders remain wary of how anything perceived as "urban" or "modern" will affect property values. I have previously argued that, in fact, by changing the system of production of suburban development, the New Urbanists are more radical than neo-avant-garde architects who change the styling of buildings but accept the fundamentals of the status quo. See Ellen Dunham-Jones, "Real Radicalism: Duany and Koolhaas," *Harvard Design Magazine*, Winter/Spring 1997, 51.

29. From a presentation by Carl Guardino of the Silicon Valley Manufacturing Group at the Congress for the New Urbanism VII, Milwaukee, June 4, 1999.

30. Paul Gottlieb, "Amenities as an Economic Development Tool: Is There Enough Evidence?" *Economic Development Quarterly*, August 1994, 276, quoted in Richard Florida, "Competition in the Age of Talent: Environment, Amenities, and the New Economy," report for the R. K. Mellon Foundation, Heinz Endowments, and Sustainable Pittsburgh (January 2000).

31. Florida, "Competition in the Age of Talent." See also Howard Gleckman, "How High Tech Can Help Save Central Cities," *Businessweek Online,* June 12, 2000; and Rebecca Bryant, "Planning for the New Economy," *Urban Land,* January 2000.

32. See Margaret Crawford, John Kaliski, and John Chase, eds., *Everyday Urbanism* (New York: Monacelli Press, 2000).

33. As reported in the *Wall Street Journal,* March 24, 1998, the International Telecommuting Association estimated there were 11.1 million telecommuters in 1997. The International Telework Association and Council estimates that today 19.6 million Americans telecommute at least one day per week; see *New York Times,* July 9, 2000, Business Section, 6. Todd A. Canter and Jacques N. Gordon report that when defined as employees working at home at least three days per week during normal business hours, telecommuting is already used by 32 percent of companies with more than 1,000 employees. Facility managers expect this number to double in three years. See "Alternative Workplace Strategies," *Wharton Real Estate Review,* Spring 1999, 21.

34. Chattanooga (Tennessee), Pasadena (California), and Kendall (Florida) are examples of cities that are retrofitting older malls to face outward to a Main Street. Newer "edge cities" such as Tysons Corner (Virginia) and Schaumberg (Illinois), as well as smaller suburban towns like Calabasos (California), Aurora (Colorado), Lenox (Kansas), Deerfield (Illinois), and Hernando Oaks (Florida) are building new town centers from scratch. Trying to encourage the clustering of activities, the New Jersey State Development and Redevelopment Plan provides seed money "for the establishing of a town center within a community that has no such center and no distinct identity at present." See www.state.nj.us/osp/doc/techfile/tfs3tool.htm; also Dirk Johnson "Town Sired by Autos Seeks Soul Downtown," *New York Times,* August 7, 1996, A8; Clifford A. Pearson, "Reworking the Mall," *Architectural Record,* March 1993.

35. Lawrence W. Cheek, "Loophole Masters," *Architecture,* June 2000, 68.

36. Based on a conversation with Simon Tomkinson, marketing director at the firm. Sienna's success in these projects stems in large part from the trust they have built up in their fifty-year experience designing retail, including big-box stores for Fred Meyer throughout the Northwest. Such work still provides the bulk of their business, but it allows them to be far more entrepreneurial in their more hybrid projects.

2

The New Urbanism and the Communitarian Trap: On Social Problems and the False Hope of Design

David Harvey

On returning to Oakland after many years of absence, Gertrude Stein remarked that "there is no there there." This is often taken as a simple condemnation of the impoverished qualities of American urban life, a comment that came naturally to someone who viewed America as her home country and Paris as her hometown. That reading fits into a long line of critical and sometimes outraged commentary on the "placelessness" and lack of "authenticity" that characterize many American cities, an urbanization process that produces what James Kunstler dubs "the geography of nowhere" (soulless suburbs, mindless edge cities, collapsing and fragmenting city cores fill in the pieces of this dyspeptic view).[1] The task of architecture and urban design is then construed as a heroic battle against such monstrous deformities. But Stein's remark was actually an intensely personal and emotional response to the rapidity of change in U.S. cities, to that process of perpetual redevelopment that obliterates and erases childhood memories of people and places. How to recuperate history, tradition, collective memory, and identity then becomes the Holy Grail.

These two themes are not necessarily mutually exclusive. And in what nowadays passes for the New Urbanism, we witness their deliberate conflation into a programmatic statement.[2] Urban living can be radically improved, made more authentic and less placeless, it is argued, by a return to concepts of neighborhood and community that once upon a time gave such vibrancy, coherence, continuity, and stability to urban life. Collective memory of a more civic past can be recaptured by a proper appeal to traditional symbols.

There is much in this movement to commend it, beyond the adrenaline surge of doing battle with conventional wisdoms entrenched in a wide range of institutions (developers, bankers, governments, transport interests, etc.). There is, first, the willingness to think about the place of particular developments within the region as a whole and to pursue a much more organic, holistic ideal of what cities and regions might be about. In so doing, the postmodern penchant for fragmentation is overcome, even as Unwin, the New York Regional Plan of 1929, and Mumford are resurrected as better guides to action than the Charter of Athens. There is, furthermore, a strong interest in intimate and integrated forms of development that bypass the rather stultifying conception of the horizontally zoned and large-platted city. This liberates an interest in the street and civic architecture as arenas of sociality. It also permits new ways of thinking about the relation between work and living, facilitates an ecological dimension to design that goes somewhat beyond the argument for superior environmental quality as a consumer good (though there is plenty of that in evidence), and begins to pay attention to the thorny problem of what to do with the profligate energy requirements of the automobile-based form of urbanization and suburbanization that has predominated in the United States since World War II.

But there is also room for skepticism. The presumption, for example, that America is "full of people who long to live in real communities, but who have only the dimmest idea of what that means in terms of physical design" betrays a certain arrogance.[3] But there are more substantive objections. It is not clear, for example, that a preference for neighborhood and community (presuming it really exists) will easily displace America's love affair with the car even if such a displacement is economically feasible. Most of the projects that have materialized, furthermore, are "greenfield" developments largely for the affluent and appear more directed to making the suburb "a better place to live" than to revitalizing decaying urban cores.[4] And it is not clear even to Vincent Scully, a skeptical ally of the movement, that the rich are really choosing "community" rather than "the image" of community.[5] Is collective memory being recaptured or invented? Even more seriously, the New Urbanism cannot get to the crux of urban impoverishment and decay. When jobs disappear, as William Julius Wilson points out in *When Work Disappears,* the whole fabric of sociality is torn asunder, making invocations of community and traditional neighborhood districts (of the sort that Andres Duany and Elizabeth Plater-Zyberk design) seem irrelevant to the fate of the "new" American metropolis actually forming all around us.[6] In the absence of employment and government largesse, the "civic" claims of the New Urbanism sound particularly hollow.

But my real worry is that the movement repeats at a fundamental level the same fallacy of the architectural and planning styles it criticizes. Put simply, does it not perpetuate the idea that the shaping of spatial order is or can be the foundation for a new moral and aesthetic order? Does it not presuppose that proper design and architectural qualities will be the saving grace not only of American cities but of social, economic, and political life in general? Few supporters of the movement would state so crude a thesis (although Kunstler comes close). Yet this presumption pervades the writings of the New Urbanists as a kind of subliminal subtext. The movement does not recognize that the fundamental difficulty with modernism was its persistent habit of privileging spatial forms over social processes. This, as Louis Marin shows, is central to all classical forms of utopianism (beginning with Sir Thomas More, whose descriptions of Utopia bear a rather distressing similarity to those set out in the New Urbanism).[7] The effect is to destroy the possibility of history and ensure social stability by containing all processes within a spatial frame. The New Urbanism changes the spatial frame but not the presumption of spatial order as a vehicle for controlling history and process.

The connection between spatial form and social process is made here through a relation between architectural design and a certain ideology of community. The New Urbanism assembles much of its rhetorical and political power through a nostalgic appeal to "community" as a panacea for our social and economic as well as our urban ills. Vincent Scully, for example, in commenting on Seaside, that icon of the New Urbanism, notes that it has "succeeded beyond any other work of architecture in our time . . . in creating an image of community, a symbol of human culture's place in nature's vastness." He continues:

> One cannot help but hope that the lessons of Seaside and of the other new towns now taking shape can be applied to the problem of housing for the poor. That is where community is most needed and where

it has been most disastrously destroyed. Center city would truly have to be broken down into its intrinsic neighborhoods if this were to take place within it. Sadly, it would all have been much easier to do before Redevelopment, when the basic structure of neighborhoods was still there. . . . It is therefore a real question whether "center city" as we know it can ever be shaped into the kind of place most Americans want to live in.[8]

The presumption here is that neighborhoods are in some sense "intrinsic," that the proper form of cities is some "structure of neighborhoods," that "neighborhood" is equivalent to "community," and that "community" is what most Americans want and need (whether they know it or not).

But can "community" really rescue us from the deadening world of social dissolution, grab-it-yourself materialism, and individualized, selfish, market-oriented greed? Community has always meant different things to different people, so what kind of "community" is understood within the philosophy of the New Urbanism? It is here that harking back to a mythological past carries its own dangerous freight.

The New Urbanism in fact connects to a facile contemporary attempt to transform large and teeming cities, so seemingly out of control, into an interlinked series of "urban villages" where, it is believed, everyone can relate in a civil and urbane fashion to everyone else. In Britain, Prince Charles has led the way on this emotional charger toward "the urban village" as the locus of urban regeneration. Leon Krier, an oft-quoted scion of the New Urbanism, is one of his key architectural outriders. And the idea attracts, drawing support from marginalized ethnic groups, impoverished and embattled working-class populations left high and dry through deindustrialization, as well as from middle- and upper-class nostalgics who view it as a civilized form of real estate development encompassing sidewalk cafés, pedestrian precincts, and Laura Ashley shops.

The darker side of this communitarianism remains unstated: from the very earliest phases of massive urbanization through industrialization, "the spirit of community" has been held as an antidote to any threat of social disorder, class war, and revolutionary violence. "Community" has ever been one of the key sites of social control and surveillance, bordering on overt social repression. Well-founded communities often exclude, define themselves against others, erect all sorts of keep-out signs (if not tangible walls). As I. M. Young points out, "Racism, ethnic chauvinism, and class devaluation . . . grow partly from the desire for community" such that "the positive identification of some groups is often achieved by first defining other groups as the other, the devalued semihuman."[9] As a consequence, community has often been a barrier to rather than facilitator of progressive social change, and much of the populist migration out of villages (both rural and urban) arose precisely because they were oppressive to the human spirit and otiose as a form of sociopolitical organization.[10] All those things that make cities so exciting—the unexpected, the conflicts, the excitement of exploring the urban unknown—will be tightly controlled and screened out with big signs that say "no deviant behavior acceptable here." No matter: the idea of the urban village or of some kind of communitarian solution to our urban ills worms its insidious way into public consciousness, with the New Urbanism as one of its forms of articulation.[11]

A more proper antidote to the underlying spatial determinism of both modernism and the New Urbanism is not to abandon all talk of the city (or even of the possibility of utopia) as a whole, but to understand urbanization as a group of fluid processes in a dialectical relation to the spatial forms to which they give rise and which in turn contain them. A utopianism of process looks very different from a utopianism of spatial form. The problem is then to enlist in the struggle to advance a more socially just, politically emancipatory, and ecologically sane mix of spatiotemporal production processes rather than to acquiesce to those imposed by uncontrolled capital accumulation, backed by class privilege and gross inequalities of political-economic power. Building something called community coupled with the politics of place can provide some sort of empowering basis for such a struggle.[12] But the New Urbanism pays no mind to that: it builds an image of community and a rhetoric of place-based civic pride and consciousness for those who do not need it, while abandoning those who do to their "underclass" fate.

The logic of capital accumulation and class privilege, though hegemonic, can never control every nuance of urbanization (let alone the discursive and imaginary space with which thinking about the city is always associated); the intensifying contradictions of contemporary urbanization, even for the privileged (some of which are highlighted in the New Urbanism), create all sorts of interstitial spaces in which liberatory and emancipatory possibilities can flourish. The New Urbanism identifies some of those spaces, but its conservatism, its communitarianism, and its refusal to confront the political economy of power blunt its revolutionary potential.

1997

Notes

1. See James Kunstler, *The Geography of Nowhere: The Rise and Decline of America's Man-Made Landscape* (New York: Simon & Schuster, 1993); and *Home from Nowhere: Remaking Our World for the Twenty-first Century* (New York: Simon & Schuster, 1996).

2. See Peter Calthorpe, *The Next American Metropolis: Ecology, Community, and the American Dream* (New York: Princeton Architectural Press, 1993); and Peter Katz, *The New Urbanism: Toward an Architecture of Community* (New York: McGraw-Hill, 1994).

3. Kunstler, *Home from Nowhere*, 43.

4. See Philip Langdon, *A Better Place to Live: Reshaping the American Suburb* (Amherst: University of Massachusetts Press, 1994).

5. See "The Architecture of Community" in Katz, *The New Urbanism*.

6. See William Julius Wilson, *When Work Disappears: The World of the New Urban Poor* (New York: Knopf, 1996).

7. See Louis Marin, *Utopics: Spatial Play* (Atlantic Highlands, NJ: Humanities Press; London: Macmillan, 1984).

8. Vincent Scully, afterword in Katz, *The New Urbanism*, 236.

9. Iris Marion Young, *Justice and the Politics of Difference* (Princeton, NJ: Princeton University Press, 1990), 311–12.

10. See, for example, Ronald Blythe, *Akenfield: Portrait of an English Village* (New York: Pantheon Books, 1969); and Richard Sennett, *The Uses of Disorder: Personal Identity and City Life* (New York: Knopf, 1970).

11. See Michael Sandel, *Liberalism and the Limits of Justice* (Cambridge; New York: Cambridge University Press, 1982), and Amitai Etzioni, *The Spirit of Community: Rights, Responsibilities, and the Communitarian Agenda* (New York: Crown Publishers, 1993) for social arguments of a similar sort.

12. I discuss this in *Justice, Nature, and the Geography of Difference* (Cambridge, MA: Blackwell Publishers, 1996).

3

Ozzie and Harriet in Hell: On the Decline of Inner Suburbs

Mike Davis

Once upon a time, a placid town, celebrated in millions of picture post-cards, basked in the golden glow of its orchards. In the 1920s it was renowned as the Queen of the Citrus Belt, with one of the highest per capita incomes in the nation. In the 1940s it was so modally middle-class—the real-life counterpart of Andy Hardy's hometown—that Hollywood used it as a preview laboratory to test audience reactions to new films. In the 1950s it became a commuter suburb for thousands of Father-Knows-Bests in their starched white shirts.

Now its nearly abandoned downtown is surrounded by acres of vacant lots and derelict homes. Its major employer, an aerospace corporation, pulled up stakes and moved to Tucson. Its police department has been embroiled in a long scandal over charges of racism and brutality. The 4H Club has been replaced by local franchises of the Crips and Bloods. Since 1970 nearly 1 percent of its population has been murdered.

"It" is Pomona, Los Angeles County's fourth largest city (population 134,000). Although geographically a suburb in outer orbit, it displays most of the pathologies typically associated with a battered inner city. What "plays in Pomona" now is mayhem and despair.

Its incidence of poverty, for example, exceeds Los Angeles', and its homicide rate, in bad years, approaches Oakland's or Baltimore's.

27

Its density of gang membership, as a percentage of the teenage male population, is one of the highest in the country. Likewise, a 1993 survey of 828 communities ranked Pomona as the eleventh worst in the nation for the welfare and health of children. In some of its schools, 80 percent of the students are poor enough to qualify for free lunches. According to 1994 statistics, one-third of Pomona Unified School District's seniors fail to graduate each year—ten times the rate of the neighboring college community of Claremont.

Years of urban renewal, meanwhile, have left its downtown as desolate as a miniature Detroit, while its proudest achievement— the tax-subsidized development of a walled, upper-income neighborhood known as Philips Ranch—has only exacerbated the sense of disenfranchisement in poorer areas like the "Island," "Sin Town," and the "Flats." Although now the mayor is a Latino (he is also a Mormon and Republican), real power in this majority Latino and black community is still firmly monopolized by the Anglo business elite—grandchildren of wealthy orchard owners—who live in the big houses "on the hill," in Ganesha Heights.

Unfortunately Pomona is not a unique case. Across the nation, hundreds of aging suburbs are trapped in the same downward spiral from garden city to crabgrass slum. It is the silent but pervasive crisis that dominates the political middle landscape.

Needless to say, the arrival of a *second* urban crisis—potentially comparable in magnitude to the seemingly endless ordeal of American inner cities—does not fit comfortably into either political party's current agenda. Although urbanists and local government researchers have been screaming at the top of their lungs for several years about the rising distress "in the inner metropolitan ring," most politicos have kept their heads buried deep in the sand.

The failure of candidates to address, or even grasp, the acuity of the suburban malaise explains, in turn, much of the populist rage that currently threatens the two-party status quo. America seems to be unraveling in its traditional moral center: the urban periphery. Indeed, the 1990 census confirms that 35 percent of suburban cities have experienced significant declines in median household income since 1980. These downward income trends in turn track the catastrophic loss of several million jobs, amplified by corresponding declines in home values and fiscal resources.

As a result, formerly bedrock "family-value" towns like Parma, Ohio (outside Cleveland), and University City, Missouri (outside St. Louis), are now experiencing the social destabilization that follows in the wake of the relentless erosion of traditional job and tax bases. As the *National Journal* tried to warn largely inattentive policy makers several years ago, "older working-class suburbs are starting to fall into the same abyss of disinvestment that their center cities did years ago." The tables have been turned.

In Southern California, of course, suburban decline is not necessarily a slow bleed. Recent aerospace and defense closures—like Hughes Missile Division's abrupt departure from Pomona, and Lockheed's abandonment of its huge Burbank complex—have had the social impact of unforeseen natural disasters. Following the Lockheed shutdown, for example, welfare caseloads in the eastern San Fernando Valley soared by 80,000 in a single eighteen-month period. In the valley as a whole (population 1.2 million), one in six residents now lives below the poverty line, and 111,000 collected unemployment checks in 1995. Gang violence has relentlessly followed in the wake of the new immiseration, and the "most dangerous street in Los Angeles," according to the LAPD, is not in South Central or East L.A. but is Blythe Street in the valley, a few blocks from the corpse of a G.M. assembly plant shut down in 1993.

But older suburbs' losses are usually someone else's gain. Just as the inner-ring suburbs once stole jobs and tax revenues from central cities, so now their pockets are being picked by the new urban centers—farther out on the spiral arms of the metropolitan galaxy—that Joel Garreau named "edge cities." It has been estimated, for example, that the inner-ring suburbs of Minneapolis–St. Paul lost 40 percent of their jobs during the 1980s to the so-called Fertile Crescent of edge cities on the metropolitan region's southwest flank. Schaumburg and central DuPage County—west of O'Hare International Airport—have had similar adverse impacts upon the older suburban communities of Cook County, as have the young edge cities of Contra Costa County upon east San Francisco Bay's traditional blue-collar suburbs.

In Los Angeles County, the eighteen-mile-long, tapeworm-shaped City of Industry puts a bizarre spin on the idea of the Edge City. It won incorporation in 1958 through the gimmick of counting mental patients in a nearby asylum as permanent residents and has had the same mayor (answering to the same small elite) for nearly thirty years. Although tiny in population (just 680, including patients), it is a superpredator in economic terms, monopolizing most of the tax assets of the southern San Gabriel Valley, including two thousand factories, warehouses, and discount outlets, as well as a world-class golf course and resort hotel. Its malign influence on surrounding, tax-starved, mainly Latino suburbs like La Puente and South El Monte (which play the role of its residential Bantustans) has been compared to an "economic atom bomb."

The edge cities, moreover, have rapidly translated their rising economic power into decisive electoral clout. Consider the astonishingly homogeneous composition of the current Republican leadership in the House. Speaker Gingrich and his top dozen lieutenants (Archer, Armey, Crane, Hyde, Kasich, and so on) represent, without a single exception, the affluent, self-contained outer suburbs—Route 290 (Houston), Las Colinas (Dallas), Schaumburg (Chicago), DuPage (Chicago), suburban Columbus, and so on—that have been the big winners in the intra-metropolitan distributional struggles of the last generation. Gingrich's Revolution, in a profound sense, has been the Edge City Revolution.

This one-sided competition between old and new suburbs has exploded latent class divisions in the historic commuter belts. Southern California, in particular, has become an unstable mosaic of such polarizations. Think of the widening socioeconomic (and ethnic) divides between northern and southern Orange County, the upper and lower tiers of the San Gabriel Valley, the east and west sides of the San Fernando Valley, and the San Fernando Valley as a whole and its "suburbs-of-a-suburb" (like Simi Valley and Santa Clarita).

Landscape amenities help shape this new metropolitan hierarchy. As a rule of thumb, Los Angeles County's affluent white suburbanites have retreated to choice foothill and beachfront communities, while the white working class has moved to new commuter 'burbs on the edge of the desert in northern Los Angeles and western San Bernardino and Riverside counties. The older 'burbs in the interior coastal plain have become majority black, Latino, and Asian. As in the San Francisco Bay region, there is permanent cold war over tax revenue and allocation of public services between the poorer "flats" and the tonier "hills."

In other metropolitan areas, of course, the class differentiation of suburbia still corresponds to the concentric rings—income increasing outward—of the old Burgess Park model of urban ecology. The "hole in the donut," as it were, is growing larger. At the same time, the new intensity of intersuburban interaction—including commutes to work and flow of goods—has dramatically weakened, if not fully displaced, the traditional solar system model of suburbs radially attracted to the center. Indeed, in some metropolises, the outlying major airport, with its office towers, warehouses, and convention facilities, has become more gravitationally important as a center of employment and exchange than the older downtown.

The have-not suburbs, moreover, have accelerated their own decline by squandering scarce tax resources in zero-sum competitions for new investment. Too many poor communities have tried to upscale themselves through a combination of draconian social engineering (restriction or even removal of low-income residents) and desperate bids for new tax resources. If a decade ago, every aging L.A. suburb from Compton to Pomona had to have its own auto mall, now the magic bullet is believed to be a card casino (and both Compton and Pomona are scheming to build one). Redevelopment programs, which in California devour 10 to 15 percent of local tax revenue, have become little more than cargo cults, praying for miraculous investments that never come.

In addition to the dramatic hemorrhage of jobs and capital over the past decade, senile suburbia also suffers from premature physical obsolescence—the architectural equivalent of Alzheimer's disease. Much of what has been built in the postwar period (and continues to be built today) is throw-away architecture, with a thirty-year or less functional lifespan. "Dingbats" and other light-frame sunbelt apartment types are especially unsuited to support the intergenerational continuity of community and property. At best, this stucco junk was designed to be promptly recycled by perennially dynamic housing markets. But such markets have stagnated or died in much of the old suburban fringe.

Now millions of units of this disposable, ticky-tacky stuff are beginning to erode into the slum housing of year 2000. Again, our Ur-suburb, the San Fernando Valley, provides a telling example. The colossal $26 billion damage inflicted by the Northridge earthquake (only a "moderate" temblor on the Richter scale) exposed some of the submerged bulk of this building-quality crisis as residents were literally killed by shoddy construction. (Disaster costs do not include the 25 percent decline in single-family home values throughout the valley since 1992: an economic catastrophe for families, exacerbated by insurance companies' refusal to provide new—legally required—earthquake coverage to homeowners.)

Although no one has yet attempted the calculation, there is little reason to suppose that this suburban "housing deficit"—the replacement cost of obsolete and unrestorable building stock—will be any smaller than Clinton's once famous but now forgotten "infrastructure deficit." Nor is it likely, as declining suburbs become the new pariahs, that the free market's invisible hand will linger longer than it takes to draw a fatal red line around their prospects for housing reinvestment. The same grim calculations apply to the neglected social infrastructure—schools, parks, libraries, and so on—created in suburbia between the 1920s and 1960s.

All of this, of course, is especially bad news for poor, inner-city residents who are being urged by every pundit in the land to find their salvation in the suburbs. Indeed, confronted with virtually Paleolithic conditions of life in collapsing city neighborhoods, hundreds of thousands of blacks and Latinos are finally finding it possible to move into the subdivisions where Beaver Cleaver and Ricky Nelson used to live. The once monochromatic San Fernando Valley, for example, now has a slight non-Anglo majority (51 to 53 percent) of Latino, black, Middle Eastern, and Asian residents, including more than 500,000 recent immigrants. There are more people of Mexican descent in Ozzie-and-Harriet Land than in East L.A.

But their experiences too often repeat the heartbreak and disillusionment of the original migrations to the central cities. What seemed from afar a promised land is at closer sight a low-rise version of the old ghetto or barrio. Like a maddening mirage, jobs and good schools are still a horizon away, in the new edge cities. The "good ole boy" regimes that hold power in the interregnum between white flight and the slow accession of new black or Latino electoral majorities usually loot every last cent in the town treasury before making their ungraceful exits. As a result, minorities typically inherit municipal scorched earth—crushing redevelopment debts, demoralized workforces, neglected schools, ghostlike business districts, and so on—as their principal legacy from the ancient regime.

In the meantime, the stranded and forgotten white populations of these transitional communities are too easily tempted to confuse structural decay with the sudden presence of neighbors of color. The vampirish role of the edge cities in sucking resources from older, more central regions of the metropolis is less immediately visible than the desperate needs of growing populations dependent upon the dole. Political discourse, moreover, constantly valorizes resentment against the poor and people of color, while remaining discreetly silent about the real structure of urban inequality. In the absence of any serious vision of reform, one of the most worrisome prospects is that new-wave racism—even some viral mutation of fascism—may yet grow legs of steel in the ruins of the suburban dream.

1997

4

Suburbia and Its Discontents: Notes from the Sprawl Debate

Matthew J. Kiefer

Most Americans don't think much about the design of the built environment, odd though this may seem to those who do. But every so often broader issues bubble up into public discourse. The debate over sprawl, until recently confined to land-use planning circles, seems to be everywhere now: at town meetings, in daily newspapers, and in latte lines at Starbucks. For most of its long etymological life, *sprawl* was only a verb: "to spread out awkwardly." The modern noun form emerged in the 1960s as the pejorative phrase "urban sprawl," reportedly coined by William H. Whyte. As the concept has gained wider cultural currency (commensurate with the awkward spread on the landscape it describes), this phrase has been shortened to a single word. Many Americans who would have difficulty naming a living architect other than Frank Gehry readily understand this meaning of *sprawl*.

"Smart Growth" has emerged as the consensus antidote. If sprawl is simply an after-the-fact description of a phenomenon, Smart Growth is a movement, a collection of environmentalists, planners, and preservationists advocating a set of land use and design strategies—although, with the exception of New Urbanism, one with no ideal physical form—intended to direct new development toward existing urbanized areas and away from agricultural and natural landscapes. The name reflects both a realization that development will occur and a desire to shape it

Cooper Carry, Mizner Park, phase one, Boca Raton, Florida, ca. 2000. Photograph courtesy of Cooper Carry.

toward positive ends. Who could oppose that? Well, many do: libertarians, property-rights advocates, suburban home builders, and, increasingly, urban residents who view Smart Growth as a move by wealthier suburbanites to shift the burdens of growth back to the city so they can continue to race to soccer games in their SUVs.

A review of the emerging literature of Smart Growth reveals both a lively internal discussion about sprawl's causes, consequences, and remedies and the beginnings of a countermovement defending the status quo as more closely reflecting American needs and values. The first generation of sprawl books geared to a wider audience, such as James Howard Kunstler's *Geography of Nowhere* (1993), Jane Holtz Kay's *Asphalt Nation* (1997), and, most recently, Andres Duany, Elizabeth Plater-Zyberk, and Jeff Speck's *Suburban Nation* (2002), are mostly of the "Ten Things I Hate about Sprawl" variety: polemics against prevailing land-use patterns and practices.

Several more recent books, reviewed for this article, form what might be called the second generation: books focused on Smart Growth solutions. For instance, *The Limitless City: A Primer on the Urban Sprawl Debate* (Washington, DC: Island Press, 2002), by Massachusetts architect Oliver Gillham, tackles the origins of sprawl, the current debate over its impacts, Smart Growth alternatives, and prospects for future directions. Though more interested in framing the debate in a balanced and thoughtful way than in staking out a rhetorical position, Gillham concludes that the consequences of sprawl are sufficiently problematic to warrant attention, through both market-based measures and government action, particularly at the state level. (If you plan to read only one book to understand the general terms of the debate, this should be it.) *Smart Growth: Form and Consequences* (Cambridge, MA: Lincoln Institute of Land Policy, 2002), edited by Massachusetts planners Terry S. Szold and Armando Carbonell, is a collection of essays by academics and practitioners on several aspects of Smart Growth. While not attempting to provide a single coherent viewpoint on Smart Growth, the book's essays are full of insights (more about these later) for those already familiar with the broad outlines of the debate.

The Regional City: Planning for the End of Sprawl (Washington, DC: Island Press, 2001), written by Sacramento architect and regional planner Peter Calthorpe and Los Angeles planner William Fulton, examines cities and suburbs as an integrated whole and uses Calthorpe's own work—designs for transit-oriented developments and regional planning and policy efforts for Portland and Salt Lake City—to describe strategies for infill development in maturing suburbs and for revitalizing older central cities. In *Solving Sprawl: Models of Smart Growth in Communities across America* (New York: National Resources Defense Council, 2001), the Natural Resources Defense Council presents sprawl as an occasion for environmental advocacy. Though reductive in its analysis of sprawl, the book's heart is a series of descriptions of thirty-five exemplary projects, grouped according to their location in cities, suburbs, and natural or rural areas.

The case against Smart Growth is increasingly being made by people associated with conservative policy institutes, such as Wendell Cox of the Heritage Foundation, Samuel Staley of the Reason Public Policy Institute, and Randal O'Toole of Oregon's Thoreau Institute. O'Toole's *The Vanishing Automobile and Other Urban Myths: How Smart Growth Will Harm American Cities* (Bandon, OR: Thoreau Institute, 2000) closes the debate circle by describing what the author hates about Smart Growth: basically everything. Grounded in his experiences in Portland, Oregon, for twenty-five years a national leader among American cities in growth control, his book energetically attacks several dozen Smart Growth "myths," including the "Myth of the Vanishing Automobile," the "Myth of the Sterile Suburbs," and the "Myth of Urban Decline" (1, 52, 214). (To dispel any lingering doubt about his intentions, O'Toole dedicates the book to "freedom fighters . . . who are working for freedom of choice, mobility, and local control.")

Of course, every debate begins with a concise statement of the problem, but it is not easy to define sprawl and its negative consequences, let alone to define Smart Growth and what distinguishes it from sprawl. Dolores Hayden's essay in *Smart Growth,* "What Is Suburbia? Naming the Layers in the Landscape, 1820–2000," advances a chronological morphology, reminiscent of John Stilgoe's and Sam Bass Warner's, of seven layers of suburbia from the first "borderlands" and "picturesque enclaves" through 1970s "edge nodes" and 1990s "e-space fringes" (19–21, 21–24, 31–33, 33–34). As Hayden points out, each of these layers (really concentric circles) still exists on the landscape, moving ever farther from the urban core in search of the triple dream of house, yard, and community.

Gillham carefully documents the origins of sprawl and particularly the effects of government policy—ranging from FHA mortgage insurance standards to federal interstate highways—in promoting sprawl. This touchstone of the anti-sprawl literature—government's role in promoting sprawl—is sometimes stretched by commentators like Hayden to suggest a conspiracy between federal officials and real estate developers to segregate social classes and increase property values. Others, including land-use attorney Brian Blaesser, another essayist in *Smart Growth,* and, more insistently, Randal O'Toole, emphasize that government policy, whether at the federal, state, or local level, more often merely honors consumer preference.

It turns out it is also not so easy to state, in a satisfying way, what is wrong with sprawl. Of course it is ugly—although Robert Venturi and Denise Scott Brown might disagree—but the Smart Growth movement struggles mightily to overcome the suspicion that it is an effort by urban aesthetes and environmentalists to impose their lifestyle choices on the majority, who generally prefer a suburban lifestyle (they just don't want so many others to like it so much too). The case against sprawl is based on its broader environmental, social, and economic impacts: its link to climate change, diminished air and water quality, and habitat and farmland destruction; its tendency to diminish community and quality of life; its increased public health costs due to respiratory ailments, traffic accidents, and even obesity—a growing problem in the United States due in part to our sedentary, auto-oriented lifestyle; the costs of extending new infrastructure to the urban fringe; and reduced productivity and other economic costs of traffic congestion.

While these linkages might seem obvious, each of them is problematic in its own way. If sprawl threatens public health, why are public health advocates largely absent from the sprawl debate? Will sprawl be acceptable if zero-emission fuel cell vehicles become widespread? Is it ultimately less costly to adjust to global warming than to reverse it? Since truly significant habitats and ecosystems are mostly preserved already by wetland protection, endangered species, flood management, and other targeted land-use controls, is the loss of natural areas per se more important than allowing human settlement to expand freely? How serious an issue is farmland preservation really, since American agricultural production continues to increase in spite of diminishing acreage under pasture or cultivation? It seems almost impossible to isolate the effects of settlement patterns among all the factors eroding community in contemporary American culture. Aren't television and the Internet more subversive? Should we regulate them instead? Since sprawl can be tamed only by revitalizing older cities, aren't the costs of rebuilding urban infrastructure likely to be at least as great as extending new infrastructure into farmland at the fringe? Isn't that part of why we avoid these costs now?

At least as difficult as defining the sprawl problem in a satisfying way is defining the Smart Growth antidote. Oliver Gillham quotes Microsoft's *Encarta World English Dictionary*'s serviceable and concise definition of Smart Growth as "economic growth that consciously seeks to avoid wastefulness and damage to the environment and communities" (158). Gillham also quotes former Maryland Governor Parris Glendening, who is widely credited with popularizing the term and who defines Smart Growth as "sensible growth that balances our need for jobs and economic development with our desire to save our natural environment" (157). Other oft-articulated Smart Growth goals include compact walkable communities; a mixture of land uses and a so-called jobs/housing balance, which reduces commuting distances; affordable housing production; and preservation of significant cultural and natural resources.

However, sometimes the term seems to be used merely as a benediction for every favored land use, design, and social policy goal. The NRDC's *Solving Sprawl* falls into this trap, articulating Smart Growth principles that include fostering attractive communities and making predictable and fair development decisions that involve community collaboration (4). These overinclusive formulations open the Smart Growth movement to criticism, not only as having a primarily social agenda and inevitably failing to achieve its lofty ambitions but also by making it almost impossible to evaluate what fraction of new development qualifies as Smart Growth.

Though it undermines Smart Growth's appeal as a paradigm shift, it seems more sensible to view growth options along a continuum from those that are more consumptive of land and resources (and, in the process, perhaps more destructive of public health and quality of life) to those that are more land- and resource-efficient (and thus tend to promote public health and quality of life). Virginia Tech professor Arthur Nelson, in an essay in *Smart Growth*, argues that developments should be evaluated against specific Smart Growth objectives to determine whether they merit the moniker and categorizes some developments and communities (for example, the DPZ-designed New Urbanist Kentlands outside Washington, DC, and the city of Boulder, Colorado, which has had an urban growth boundary since 1978) as "better growth" but not good enough to be Smart Growth. Part of an emerging effort to develop "indicators" of sprawl and Smart Growth, this evaluation suggests a baseline against which alternatives can be measured, although that is not so easy to establish either.

An example of the problem on a small scale involves the width of new residential streets. The fifty- to sixty-foot width recommended by the Institute of Transportation Engineers for the past half century is now widely viewed as promoting excessive impervious surface, unnecessary land consumption, and the exaltation of fire access above all other goals. MIT professor Eran Ben-Joseph's essay in *Smart Growth* includes a table of smarter standards from cities around the country ranging from twenty- to twenty-two-feet widths for streets with parking on one side to between twenty-eight and thirty-four feet for streets with parking on both sides (116–17). Is a twenty-eight-foot street always "smarter" than a thirty-four-foot street? At what point between thirty-four and fifty feet have we shaded from Smart Growth into sprawl?

Thankfully, the many examples of thoughtful planning and development described by Calthorpe, Gillham, and the NRDC remind us not to get too bogged down in a semantic debate. For instance, recycling the American Can Company's industrial complex in the Canton neighborhood of Baltimore into an office, retail, and restaurant complex, with the support of Maryland's Smart Growth program, seems a clearly preferable outcome to having this growth occur at a suburban highway interchange or even to a previous proposal to demolish the late-nineteenth-century buildings and construct two high-rise residential towers. (Neighborhood opposition defeated this.) If Smart Growth can become a rallying cry—and, in Maryland at least, a source of funding—for better outcomes like this, how can it be bad? Similarly, Calthorpe's "Crossings" neighborhood in Mountain View, California, located near a supermarket, a department store, and a newly opened Caltrans station between San Jose and San Francisco, contains about four hundred housing units mixed among single-family houses, townhouses, and apartments. It is difficult to argue that this is not an improvement over the failed mall it replaces.

Of course, the libertarian position would dispute that these outcomes warrant limiting freedom of choice. O'Toole claims that since only 5 percent of the country's total land area is now developed, there is plenty left for future population growth even at low densities. In fact, this is a difficult assertion to prove or disprove, based as it is on assumptions about the amount of undeveloped land that is developable at all, the likely rate of population growth, increases in agricultural productivity, and the limits to commuting distances as urban areas atomize. Other libertarian critiques seem more obtuse: for instance, the assertion that because air quality is worse in urban than in suburban areas, Smart Growth actually diminishes air quality. Not content merely to question whether the scope of the sprawl problem warrants compromising other deeply held American values, the libertarian critique tries to refute every tenet of the Smart Growth movement as factually unproven or philosophically misguided. It perhaps tries to prove too much, without acknowledging that its own position is a form of social engineering, too, just with different goals in mind.

A lively debate exists both within and outside the Smart Growth movement over which mechanisms are most effective to achieve it. As Harvard professor Jerold Kayden points out in his clear-eyed essay in *Smart Growth,* the U.S. Supreme Court has left the states wide latitude in choosing whether or how to adopt growth controls. Some—most notably Oregon—in the 1970s chose urban growth boundaries administered by regional government with far-reaching, though sometimes controversial results. (They create winners and losers by making land within the boundary more valuable than land outside it.) No large cities other than Portland have adopted them, and the smaller ones that have often lack the regional authority over land use and transportation decisions necessary to fulfill their purposes.

Maryland's Smart Growth program takes a more incentive-based approach: it directs state aid for roads, sewers, and schools to existing urbanized areas and provides funding for open space acquisition, farmland preservation, and brownfields redevelopment. Adopted in 1995, the program is still too new to evaluate. Perhaps more troubling, its champion, former Governor Parris Glendening, was succeeded in January 2003 by Bob Ehrlich, a Republican whose commitment to the program is uncertain at best. A host of other measures trumpeted at Smart Growth conferences, including cluster zoning, community land trusts, more compact New Urbanist development, and bicycle and walking paths funded through the federal Transportation Efficiency Act, reduce the pace of sprawl only marginally, without materially changing land use and development patterns.

A lively debate is also going on about the effects of digital technology on sprawl. As William Mitchell writes in *Smart Growth*, every new type of infrastructure loosens spatial linkages. Just as piped water diminished the importance of proximity to the village well, new communications technology allows corporations to locate their call centers in India and allows employees to telecommute, thus, perhaps, lowering traffic congestion but increasing decentralization. Digital television makes home entertainment more appealing, maybe reducing vehicle trips for movies and concerts. E-retailing, though reducing shopping excursions, replaces private automobile trips with delivery truck trips; this may work at cross-purposes with the move to narrower, more pedestrian-friendly residential streets. Freed from the tyranny of geography, people can choose to live in the most livable places, converting sites from manufacturing centers to lifestyle venues where social interaction is by choice rather than by chance. Does this foster less community or more?

The reader strains to draw firm conclusions from this bewildering variety of viewpoints on sprawl and Smart Growth. Human settlement seems to spread inexorably as population grows and technology advances. The region is now well established as the basic spatial settlement unit, yet land use, for the most part, continues to be regulated at the local level. Sprawl can thus be viewed as a consequence of an effectively unregulated land market, aided by government tax and transportation policy. It will be reduced only if Americans choose to give government a mandate to use basic powers of regulation, taxation, and spending to intervene in the marketplace to serve important public policy goals, just as it did to build interstate highways, create a federal system of mortgage insurance favoring single-family homes, and offer a mortgage-interest deduction. All of these deliberate governmental actions responded to powerful popular wishes and were extraordinarily successful in achieving their goals. Americans enjoy levels of home ownership, mobility, and economic prosperity unknown in history. On these matters, the suburban experiment must be pronounced a resounding success.

As with other raging successes, however, suburbia suffers from the failings of its virtues. In our continual, poignant quest to achieve a pastoral ideal based on privacy, economic security, and mobility, we have converted concentric borderlands into the thing they once bordered, with mounting secondary consequences, and it is not clear that we have yet reached a turning point. Enormous private and public capital costs have been sunk into existing low-density suburban development. It seems foolhardy to count on igniting a mass outbreak of altruism to change this, as more evangelical Smart Growth advocates sometimes do, even if altruism is often merely an appeal to longer-term self-interest. Americans tend to venerate mobility and freedom of choice and are likely to limit them only when it increases their economic security within a comprehensible time frame.

Zoning became accepted in the early decades of the twentieth century mainly to protect homeowners from industrial and commercial expansion. Its effect was, on balance, to increase property values, even if some individual owners suffered. Smart Growth has already taken root where it has a similar effect. For instance, most smaller communities that have adopted urban growth boundaries—including Boulder, Colorado; Lancaster County, Pennsylvania; and Keene, New Hampshire—are places with a small industrial base where second homes and tourism, and thus aesthetic appeal, are economic engines. What will it take for more Americans to perceive it in their economic interest to change their ways?

Of course, rapid change could be brought about by a galvanizing event—the way nuclear power's upward trajectory was halted by the accident at Three Mile Island in 1979. One or more large-scale environmental breakdowns traceable to overly consumptive land-use practices could lead to concerted action if they cause serious economic dislocation. Security concerns in the wake of the September 11, 2001, terrorist attacks may be exerting another centrifugal force on central cities. Other factors, such as our increasing global environmental footprint, seem less likely to force change. As Gillham points out, with only 5 percent of the planet's population, the United States consumes 35 percent of the world's transportation energy. But Americans show no signs of greater willingness to curb consumption in response to international pressure to address global climate change. It also seems unlikely that the world's oil reserves will be depleted before alternative-fuel vehicles are widely available, forcibly reducing auto dependence. Although some Smart Growth advocates emphasize that suburbanization's tendency to concentrate poverty in central cities could lead to social unrest, at least two recent studies of 2000 census data show that poverty has become less concentrated, not more, since 1990.[1]

While it may be more engrossing to speculate about world-changing events, it seems more likely that change will come incrementally because of a factor that is much more mundane: consumer preference. As commuting distances increase, cities from Boston to Bilbao are reinventing themselves with notable success as lifestyle venues, based in large part on providing a more pedestrian-friendly, culturally rich environment. This has little to do, really, with environmental protection or threats to public health, but it is unwise to underestimate the power of the consumer, which produced suburbs in the first place.

Democracy—consumer preference writ large—unfailingly reflects the popular will. Its self-correcting mechanism is reactive, nonlinear, and certainly imperfect, but it does provide some comfort that if sprawl is as outmoded as many are coming to believe, sprawl will have to change.

2004

Notes

1. Robert Pear, "Smaller Percentage of Poor Live in High-Poverty Areas," *New York Times,* May 18, 2003, 20, describing studies by Paul A. Jargowsky of the University of Texas and G. Thomas Kingsley and Kathryn L. S. Pettit of the Urban Institute.

5

The Costs—and Benefits?—
of Sprawl

Alex Krieger

In the growing literature on sprawl, a predominant view holds urban sprawl accountable for much that is wrong with America. This is the view of New Urbanists, among others, who consider sprawl a recent and aberrant form of urbanization that threatens even the American Dream. Such is clearly expressed in titles such as *Suburban Nation: The Rise of Sprawl and the Decline of the American Dream* (2000) by Andreas Duany, Elizabeth Plater-Zyberk, and Jeff Speck, and *The Regional City: Planning for the End of Sprawl* (2001) by their West Coast counterparts Peter Calthorpe and William Fulton.[1]

A second view—today less often expressed by planners or the media— is that the effort to control sprawl is an elitist attack on the American Dream, an attack that withholds that dream from those who are still trying to fulfill it. Its current spokesmen are libertarians and others opposed to further government restrictions on property rights.

While opposition to sprawl is growing, the motivations for this opposition are complex and occasionally contradictory. And while support for, or acquiescence to, sprawl generally comes from those fighting to maintain unencumbered property rights, their reassertion of the benefits of sprawl—benefits that motivated most American land development in the first place—cannot be as easily dismissed as sprawl opponents assert.

But what constitutes sprawl? That simple word carries the burden

Los Angeles skyline at dusk as seen from Griffiths Park, ca. 2000. Photograph by Walter Bibikow/Taxi.

of representing the highly complex set of effects from low-density urban expansion. Humanity is still urbanizing, with cities worldwide spreading outward at unprecedented rates, but in North America, sprawl, though not literally synonymous with suburbanization, generally refers to suburban-style, auto-dominated, zoned-by-use development spread thinly over a large territory, especially in an "untidy" or "irregular" way.[2] Among the oldest and most persistent critiques of American urban sprawl centers on this visual awkwardness and conjures up an image of the human body sprawling.

Mainstream media attention to sprawl has increased dramatically in recent years. Indeed, in the two years that straddled the millennium, sprawl was the subject of lengthy articles in such publications as the *Atlantic Monthly, Harper's, National Geographic, Scientific American,* and *Time* and of several front-page stories in *USA Today*—an impressive attention to land use by media that generally ignore the subject. Scores of other "something-must-be-done-about-sprawl" features, including two Ted Koppel *Nightline* shows, appeared during the period. *Preservation Magazine* even chimed in with a long essay on "Golf Sprawl."[3] On the heels of (and perhaps because of) a decade of prosperity, and as Americans faced a new century, the media identified sprawl as that condition of urbanization that was producing—and if allowed to continue would rapidly accelerate—an erosion in Americans' quality of life. A seductive sound bite to counter sprawl also continued to gain prominence: "Smart Growth." Around this mantra gather environmentalists, proponents of urban reinvestment, advocates of social equity, preservationists, spokesmen for various "livability agendas,"[4] public housing officials, and a few trend-sensitive developers, all rallying against, well, sprawl. At the turn of the millennium, virtually all who consider themselves enlightened about land use and environmental stewardship concur that sprawl is bad for America.

More recent concerns about security and a weaker economy have shifted public and media attention but have not relegated discussion of sprawl back to planning journals. Indeed, one of the worries among city advocates immediately following the events of September 11, 2001, was a reacceleration of suburbanization—of people and businesses seeking "safer" places to live and work than terrorist-target areas like Manhattan. This reaction has a precedent during the Cold War, when the threat of nuclear holocaust produced similar concerns, launching campaigns for "defensive dispersion." In the late 1940s and early 1950s, planning journals (and scientific journals like *Bulletin of the Atomic Scientists*) regularly published articles like "The Dispersal of Cities as a Defensive Measure" and "A Program for Urban Dispersal."[5]

I will return to the arguments periodically made on behalf of sprawl. But what are the arguments against it? There are five principal lines of critique:

The oldest is aesthetic, though not often recognized as such. Recall the "ticky-tacky houses" folk songs of the 1960s and, earlier still, the damning words of a poet, relevant still three-quarters of a century later: "I think I shall never see / A billboard lovely as a tree / Perhaps, unless the billboards fall, / I'll never see a tree at all."[6] While there is a trace of ecological concern in these lines by Ogden Nash, for many, even those lacking poetic sensibilities, the physical environments produced by miles of low-density settlement are simply ugly. They disfigure and insult both nature and worthier examples of human artifice. Among the most effective tactics used by New Urbanists is to simply produce images of prettier environments—recalling the charms but never the limitations of old small towns. Such Currier and Ives vignettes of the future (rather than, as the originals portrayed, of scenes of rapidly disappearing vernacular traditions) help persuade some that the character of places vanished can be recovered to replace the visual chaos of the contemporary suburban landscape. Whether the dressing up of the suburb in townlike iconography can actually diminish sprawl remains to be proven. It seems unlikely that more attractive or somewhat more compact subdivisions would significantly reduce Americans' appetite for roaming far and wide in search of necessities or amusements.

The second argument is sociological. Already in the 1950s, critics like William H. Whyte and John Keats portrayed suburban life as conformist, drab, and isolationist.[7] In the decades since, such arguments have expanded to suggest correlations between suburbanization and social apathy and intolerance of neighbors unlike oneself. Concerns are voiced about alienated suburban youth, dependent on parent chauffeurs to get anywhere, about the enslavement of parents to their chauffeur role, and about the isolation of grandparents who can no longer drive themselves. Apprehension about the social isolation of suburban stay-at-home moms has gradually shifted to sociologists' worry about the difficulties of combining careers and child rearing across a dispersed landscape. The title of Robert Putnam's recently popular *Bowling Alone* implies that privation of group activity is also a consequence of lives spent in sprawled, disconnected America, although Putnam admits that he could draw only circumstantial correlations between sprawl and a decline in civic engagement.[8]

The third critique is environmental and is certainly the most compelling. This critique has slowly (far too slowly for some) gained power since the late 1960s and early 1970s, when Rachel Carson's *Silent Spring*, Ian McHarg's *Design with Nature,* the first Earth Day, and publications such as *The Limits to Growth* and *The Costs of Sprawl* helped arouse profound concern about human abuses of the environment.[9] Although worldwide environmental degradation has many causes, sprawl is a major contributor. Few can argue that low-density development does not increase auto emissions, water use, pollution, trash, loss of species habitat, and energy consumption. To cite one example, most pollution of groundwater, lakes, streams, and rivers in the United States is caused by runoff that collects various toxins on the high percentage of impervious surfaces, like roads and parking lots, in urbanized regions. The heating and cooling of free-standing homes, with their many exterior walls per capita, require more energy than does attached, denser development. And then there are those immaculate lawns that require ample water and chemicals to maintain. Of course, most such conditions are caused by increasing affluence, not just settlement patterns. Affluence and sprawl are not unrelated. Environmentalists have become among the fiercest critics of sprawl, armed with sobering statistics and demanding reform. The first issue in 2000 of *Sierra,* the magazine of the Sierra Club, devoted itself entirely to the arrival of what it called "The Green Millennium," which various authors said needed to be freer of sprawl.[10] There is little doubt that calls for better environmental stewardship—leading to legislated restrictions on development—will increase in the coming decades, influencing urbanization patterns considerably.

The fourth argument is that sprawl breeds boring "lifestyles." In addition to dyed-in-the-wool urbanists (like me), some among the generation of now-grown children of Baby Boomers, having been raised in the suburbs, are pining for more convivial surroundings. Precisely what proportion feel this way is hard to establish, but various informal housing preference surveys along with the modest recent rise in demand for downtown housing provide considerable anecdotal evidence. A century ago rural populations were lured to cities mainly by economic opportunity. Now younger adults, less inclined to follow in the footsteps of their suburbia-pioneering parents, seek out the cultural and social stimulation of city life. Think of the sultry allure of New York in the TV series *Sex and the City.* By comparison, where is the action along Boston's "Technology Highway," Route 128, once the day's work of inventing or investing is done? Rarely does one find fine dancing or music clubs among the Blockbusters, Burger Kings, and karaoke bars of suburbia. Young Americans find city life exotic, even as child-rearing years and the accompanying search for better public schools and affordable housing return most to the comforts of suburbia. Back in the suburbs, young parents lament how hard interesting lives are to create amid the sprawl.

The fifth case against sprawl, becoming more prevalent, is self-protection. Outwardly it is waged as a campaign, mostly in affluent communities, against loss of open space and growing traffic congestion. Its underlying stance is less noble, constituting some variation of "don't harm my lifestyle by replicating the locational decisions I made a few years earlier; your arrival will ruin my lovely neighborhood." As David Brooks, author of *Bobos in Paradise,* noted in a recent *New York Times* article about exurban voters, "Even though they often just moved to these places, exurbanites are pretty shameless about trying to prevent more people from coming after them."[11] On one level, this is understandable. No one wants one's access to nature obstructed or one's commute lengthened. However, such a "Not in My Back Yard" attitude pushes development away from areas resisting growth, increasing rather than containing sprawl. New subdivisions simply leapfrog to the next exit along the highway, where less expensive land (along with fewer constraints on development) is available. Once settled, these newcomers will guard against subsequent encroachers.

While anti-sprawl literature relying on one or more of these positions receives substantial attention, little fanfare accompanied the recent publication of a rare rebuttal. In 2001, Randal O'Toole, expressing views that have traditionally been mainstream—and may, indeed, still be—published *The Vanishing Automobile and Other Urban Myths*, subtitled *How Smart Growth Will Harm American Cities*.[12] The book's sensibility seems entirely out of kilter with the times. Reading him raises one's sprawl-busting dander, yet its copiously assembled statistics are impressive, if hard to corroborate.

The book calls many of the core assumptions advanced by the critics of sprawl myths. For example, while Jane Holtz Kay's *Asphalt Nation,* a characteristic condemnation of sprawl, cites numerous (equally hard to substantiate) statistics about what she calls "the cost of the car culture," O'Toole asserts that, on a passenger per mile basis, public dollars in support of transit are double what they are for highways.[13] Determining in precise monetary terms how much our culture subsidizes auto usage is nearly impossible. We certainly *favor* car usage and thus, no doubt, support and benefit from direct and many indirect subsidies. Still, within the narrow terms of how he frames the issue—passenger per mile costs—O'Toole makes his point: since most of us use cars and few of us use public transit, the *public* investment in public transit *per user* is plausibly higher than the public investment *per user* for highways. This does not mean (although O'Toole so argues) that it is not sound public policy to invest in public transit or to raise the cost of driving.

Public subsidy of auto usage is but one of the seventy-three (!) myths that O'Toole identifies in what he calls the "The War against the Suburbs."[14] He criticizes the much admired experiment in regional growth management in Portland, Oregon, by pointing out (as others are) the rise in housing costs in the center of the city and that light-rail system extensions have reduced the number of neighborhood bus lines. He concludes that both changes disproportionably affect the poor and thus questions the social equity arguments advanced by transit proponents and growth boundary advocates. He quantifies the substantial preference that Americans at almost all social and economic levels continue to show for larger homes, less density, more open space, and the personal wealth generation that home ownership has brought. He debunks the assertion that new highways increase congestion by attracting additional traffic (first claimed by Lewis Mumford in the 1950s[15]) by asserting that over the past two decades, while the number of auto miles traveled has nearly doubled, the number of road miles has increased by less than 3 percent. He has the temerity to suggest that people *like* to drive and are not *forced* to drive by an absence of alternatives. He points out that less than 5 percent of the land area of the continental United States is urbanized, so fears of running out of land are premature. He argues that it is density, not dispersion, that causes congestion and offers statistics that the densest American cities have the worst incidence of congestion and often the longest commutes. In a characteristic dig at conventional Smart Growth wisdom, which supports density and opposes highways, he writes: "The Los Angeles metropolitan area is the epitome of smart growth, as it has the highest density and the fewest miles of freeway per capita of any U.S. urbanized area."[16]

To anyone whose values or intuitions align with current critiques against sprawl, O'Toole's conclusions seem either irresponsible or naively contrarian. Of course, the arguments for and against sprawl are not going to be resolved by competing value-laden statistics. As the furious debate fueled by the publication of Bjørn Lomborg's *The Skeptical Environmentalist* illustrates, ideology and polemical bias can bend many a statistic.[17] Ignoring O'Toole's stance, nonetheless, disregards the fact that for much of American history, sprawl (though not called that) was considered progressive—a measure of citizens' socioeconomic advancement.

Prior to the concern about population concentrations brought about by the atomic bomb—during the 1930s, for example—President Roosevelt's Resettlement Administration was committed to sprawl, then called *decentralization*. It was seen as one means for recovering from the Great Depression and preventing similar economic setbacks in the future.[18] A widely held assumption was that among the causes of the Depression were unwieldy and unmanageable concentrations of commerce, capital, and power. In other words, many concluded that huge unmanageable cities (like New York) were partially to blame.

Two generations earlier, Henry George, writing in *Progress and Poverty*, predicted that concentration of urban populations would worsen economic inequality. He argued passionately that social inequality was endemic to cities, where overcrowding and land possession by the few perpetuated poverty. His "remedies" were to eliminate all private land ownership (impractical, of course) and to disperse urban populations, so that "the people of the city would thus get more of the pure air and sunshine of the country, and the people of the country more of the economic and social life of the city."[19] For George's many followers, and the American advocates of the slightly later Garden City Movement, the road away from inequality led out of cities. This argument echoes today in the continuing migration from older urban centers of people in search of economic upward mobility.

The affirmation of population decentralization can be traced in a straight intellectual line to America's founding fathers, in particular to the persuasive Thomas Jefferson. Fearing the consequences of America becoming urban, Jefferson went so far as to invent a land-partitioning policy that he hoped would negate the need for urban concentrations. For Jefferson, cities were corrupting, even "pestilential" influences, and government support for the small landowner—dispersed on his self-sufficient homestead—was crucial to America's future.[20]

Jefferson's worries about urbanization seemed prescient to those witnessing the unprecedented urban concentrations of the later part of the nineteenth century and early part of the twentieth. At the turn of the twentieth century, daily life in New York's Lower East Side, depicted in Jacob Riis's photojournalism and like life in the London slums of Charles Dickens's novels, offered little hope for improving the human condition. What seemed problematic about contemporary urbanization prior to the mid-twentieth century (and what remains problematic in much of the developing world) was concentration. And sprawl, although called by various less tarnished names, was advocated as a partial solution.

Thus, by the time the middle class sprawled outside cities in great numbers in the decades following World War II, widespread public optimism about the results prevailed, despite an occasional dissent from a William H. Whyte or a Lewis Mumford. It is eerie now to read Whyte's 1958 (!) essay in *Fortune* titled *"Urban Sprawl,"* or John

Keats's 1957 novel *A Crack in the Picture Window,* or Peter Blake's 1963 *"The Suburbs Are a Mess"* in *The Saturday Evening Post.*[21] Many of the aesthetic and social arguments against sprawl (the ecological concern arose about a decade later) were already well enumerated, or at least anticipated, a half century ago. Very few citizens were paying much attention, however. Quite happily, and by the millions, Americans sought out the comforts, spatial expanse, clean air, economic leverage, and *novelty* of the Levittowns and their various imitations. At mid-twentieth century, sprawl was considered good for Americans and the nation.

What then has made that optimism (a fulfillment of the Jeffersonian ideal) wane, and *has* it truly waned?[22] Are Americans actually adjusting their image of the good life and its setting? Perhaps, but what has mostly changed is individuals' perception of the impact on them of others' sprawl. What has changed is the quantity of sprawlers and the sheer scale of their sprawling.

In the half century since 1950, the spread of sprawl has been exponential. Urban populations slightly more than doubled, while the land area used by this population has increased by a factor of four! In the Los Angeles area the factor has been seven! Two million acres of farmland and open space have been, and are continuing to be, lost to development every year. Cars have multiplied twice as fast as the population. Estimates of the costs of time lost and fuel wasted in traffic range into the billions of dollars per year. Ozone-alert days in sprawled metro areas such as Atlanta and Phoenix have been rising for decades, despite improved auto emissions and other environmental controls. North Americans currently use the equivalent of ten acres of land per capita, whereas less developed countries use approximately one acre per capita.[23]

Such disturbing statistics have only recently unsettled the complacency of suburbanites, or wannabe ones, who heretofore believed that by simply moving farther out they could avoid the personal inconveniences caused by the sprawl. For most Americans, it has always been easier to retreat than to repair. This has led to schizophrenic urbanism—people making new places that evoke old qualities while being oblivious to the consequences of abandoning exemplary places made earlier. This self-perpetuating cycle of American urbanization—expanding rings of new development, disinvestments in settled areas, wasteful consumption of resources, obsolescence, highway congestion, economic (now more than racial) segregation, homogeneity, always leading to new cycles of perimeter development—is finally being acknowledged as self-defeating.

What has begun to rattle Americans is the awareness that once all of us got "out there," some of the advantages of "getting away" have proven illusive. This, however, does not mean that Americans believe that such advantages are no longer worth pursuing, as Randal O'Toole and *USA Today* remind us. In a recent *USA Today* survey giving people four choices of ideal living circumstances, 51 percent chose a 100-year-old farm on ten acres, 30 percent chose a five-bedroom Tudor in the suburbs, and 10.5 percent selected a Beverly Hills mansion. This left a mere 8.5 percent choosing a designer loft in Manhattan.[24] No, Americans have not yet abandoned their sprawling instinct, but they are developing a lower tolerance for the sprawl of their neighbors. This is generally unacknowledged in the waves of anti-sprawl literature (which my wife has labeled "the scrawl about sprawl").

What must be brought to the fore in the debate over sprawl is this: the benefits of sprawl—for example, more housing for less cost with higher eventual appreciation—still tend to accrue to Americans individually, while sprawl's cost in infrastructure building, energy generation, and pollution mitigation tends to be borne by society overall. Understanding this imbalance is essential, and seeking ways to adjust to whom and how the costs and benefits of sprawl accrue remains the real challenge. Can political will be developed on behalf of impact fees, user assessments, regional tax-sharing, higher gasoline taxes and highway tolls, streamlined permitting and up-zoning in already developed areas, ceilings on mortgage deductions, surcharges on second homes, open space (and related) amenity assessments, regional transfer-of-development rights, and similar ideas that may shift some of the costs of sprawl onto the sprawlers? There is insufficient evidence for this today, but there is hope that the growing awareness of sprawl's liabilities will lead to such policies.

Yes, continuing the scrawl against sprawl is worthwhile. However, the goal of creating a more diverse, life-enriching, and environmentally sound urban future will ultimately depend on Americans finding ways to align short-term self-interest with long-term social value. This is not as naive as its sounds, nor is it a plea for altruism. As the bursting of the New Economy stock market bubble taught many of us, pursuit of short-term gains can backfire. A larger perspective seems needed, which in this case means recognizing that the cost—and any benefits—of sprawl must be more equitably shared.

2004

Notes

1. Andres Duany, Elizabeth Plater-Zyberk, and Jeff Speck, *Suburban Nation: The Rise of Sprawl and the Decline of the American Dream* (New York: North Point Press, 2000); Peter Calthorpe and William Fulton, *The Regional City: Planning for the End of Sprawl* (Washington, DC: Island Press, 2001).

2. *The New Oxford American Dictionary* definition of *sprawl* emphasizes such ungainly, irregular, awkward conditions.

3. Bruce Katz and Jennifer Bradley, "Divided We Sprawl," *Atlantic Monthly*, December 1999, 26–42; John G. Mitchell, "Urban Sprawl," *National Geographic*, July 2001, 48–71; Donald D. T. Chen, "The Science of Smart Growth," *Scientific American*, December 2000, 84–91; Richard Lacayo, "The Brawl over Sprawl," *Time*, March 22, 1999, 44–48; James Morgan, "Golf Sprawl," *Preservation Magazine*, May/June 2001, 38–47, 115.

4. In 1998, during the early phases of Vice President Al Gore's presidential bid, he published a policy document called *"Clinton-Gore Livability Agenda: Building Livable Communities for the Twenty-first Century."* For various reasons (including the supposition that it did not catch on with the electorate), the Smart Growth part of his campaign became less and less pronounced over the course of the campaign.

5. Tracy B. Augur, "The Dispersal of Cities as a Defensive Measure," *Journal of the American Institute of Planners*, Summer 1948, 29–35; Donald and Astrid Monson, "A Program for Urban Dispersal," *Bulletin of the Atomic Scientists* 7, 1951, 244–50. One recent essay has carefully reviewed such dispersal strategies from midcentury: Michael Quinn Dudley, "Sprawl as Strategy: City Planners Face the Bomb," *Journal of Planning Education and Research 21*, 2001, 52–63.

6. Ogden Nash, *The Pocket Book of Ogden Nash* (New York: Little Brown, 1962). By coincidence, 1962 also was the year of Malvina Reynolds's famous folk song "Little Boxes," "They're all made out of ticky-tacky, and they all look just the same."

7. William H. Whyte, "Urban Sprawl," *Fortune*, January 1958, 102–9. The term *urban sprawl* may have been coined with this essay. John Keats, *The Crack in the Picture Window* (New York: Houghton-Mifflin, 1957). Keats's novel so railed against the disfunctionalities of suburban lifestyles that he compared suburbia to the urban nightmare in George Orwell's *1984*.

8. Robert D. Putnam, *Bowling Alone: The Collapse and Revival of Ameri-*

can Community (New York: Simon & Schuster, 2000). Putnam postulates several causes for an increase in civic disengagement but concludes: "Yet [sprawl] cannot account for more than a small fraction of the decline, for civic disengagement is perfectly visible in smaller towns and rural areas as yet untouched by sprawl" (215).

9. The first Earth Day was held in 1970. Rachel Carson, *Silent Spring* (New York: Fawcett Crest, 1962); Ian McHarg, *Design with Nature* (New York: National History Press, 1969); Donella H. Meadows, Dennis L. Meadows, Jørgen Randers, William W. Behrens III, *The Limits to Growth: A Report for the Club of Rome's Project on the Predicament of Mankind* (New York: Signet, 1972); Real Estate Research Corporation. *The Costs of Sprawl in Detailed Cost Analysis* (Washington, DC: U.S. Government Printing Office, 1974).

10. Curbing sprawl was one of "five bold ideas for the new century" offered in the January/February 2000 issue of *Sierra*.

11. David Brooks, "For Democrats, Time to Meet the Exurban Voter," *New York Times,* November 10, 2002, 3.

12. Randal O'Toole, *The Vanishing Automobile and Other Urban Myths: How Smart Growth Will Harm American Cities* (Bandon, OR: Thoreau Institute, 2001).

13. Jane Holtz Kay, *Asphalt Nation: How the Automobile Took Over America and How We Can Take It Back* (New York: Crown Publishers, 1997); and O'Toole, *The Vanishing Automobile,* 117.

14. O'Toole, *The Vanishing Automobile,* 37.

15. Lewis Mumford first addressed the car as a "destroyer of cities" in the 1945 publication *City Development* and expanded the argument in the article "The Highway and the City," published in *Architectural Record* in April 1958. He devoted considerable attention to the issue in his classic *The City in History: Its Origins, Its Transformation, and Its Prospects* (New York: Harcourt Brace Jovanovich Publishers, 1961), and most vehemently in *The Highway and the City* (Westport, CT: Greenwood Press, 1981, first published 1963).

16. O'Toole, *The Vanishing Automobile,* 392.

17. Bjørn Lomborg, *The Skeptical Environmentalist: Measuring the Real State of the World* (Cambridge and New York: Cambridge University Press, 2001); and *Scientific American,* "Misleading Math about the Earth: Science Defends Itself against *The Skeptical Environmentalist,*" January 2002. Lomborg's book, the lengthy critiques published by four scientists in *Scientific American,* and Lomborg's rebuttal to these critiques unleashed a virtual firestorm of other rebuttals, and an occasional essay in Lomborg's defense, in scores of popular and scientific environmental journals and across the Internet, a firestorm that continues to this day.

18. An often repeated statement attributed to Rexford G. Tugwell, President Roosevelt's first administrator of the Resettlement Administration, spoke

directly to the hopes for decentralization: "To go just outside centers of population, pick up cheap land, build a whole new community and entice people into it. Then go back into the cities and tear down whole slums and make parks of them." Quoted in Arthur Schlesinger Jr., *The Age of Roosevelt: The Coming of the New Deal* (Boston: Houghton Mifflin, 1958), 370.

19. Henry George, *Progress and Poverty: An Inquiry into the Cause of Industrial Depressions and of Increase of Want with Increase in Wealth: A Remedy,* first published in 1879 (New York: Robert Schalkenbach Foundation, 1981), 127.

20. Thomas Jefferson often expressed his concerns about a future urbanized America. A typical example is found in a letter to James Madison written in 1787: "I think our government will remain virtuous for many centuries; . . . as long as there shall be vacant land in any part of America. When they get piled upon one another in large cities, as in Europe, they will become corrupt as in Europe." Quoted in A. Whitney Griswald, "The Agrarian Democracy of Thomas Jefferson," *The American Political Science Reader,* August 1946, 668.

21. W. H. Whyte, "Urban Sprawl"; John Keats, *The Crack in the Picture Window*; Peter Blake, "The Suburbs Are a Mess," *The Saturday Evening Post,* October 5, 1963.

22. One would think that optimism has waned when one reads a report such as "Beyond Sprawl: New Patterns of Growth to Fit the New California," sponsored by Bank of California (along with several environmental and housing advocacy organizations), first published in 1995 and widely distributed since then. The executive summary begins with the following sentence: "Ironically, unchecked sprawl has shifted from an engine of California's growth to a force that now threatens to inhibit growth and degrade the quality of life."

23. Statistics gathered from the 2000 U.S. Census, http://quickfacts.census.gov/qfd.

24. *USA Today,* "Country Calls: Where Americans Say They Would Live If Money or Circumstances Were Not an Issue," August 27, 2002, 1.

6

Smart Growth in Atlanta: A Response to Krieger and Kiefer

Ellen Dunham-Jones

Living in Atlanta, a city whose reputation as the poster child for sprawl precipitated significant ongoing public and private "Smart Growth" initiatives, I have "situated knowledge" of specific examples to both corroborate and question Alex Krieger's and Matthew Kiefer's more general comments on the discourse on sprawl and Smart Growth. As both authors point out, Smart Growth is difficult to define precisely. Atlanta's attempts to put Smart Growth into practice reveal an even messier, one-step-forward, two-steps-back, multipronged effort involving U.S. government–pressured regional planning on the one hand, and market-driven individual development projects on the other. The marriages and divorces of environmentalists, business leaders, and planners have made for strange bedfellows and unintended political consequences. Successes and failures have occurred at both the regional and the project scales. The battle against sprawl is not being won— yet—(nor is Smart Growth likely to alter the vast established physical pattern[1]), but its multiple manifestations have already succeeded in providing Atlantans with a much broader array of living, working, and transportation choices.

Krieger and Kiefer make similar points about the wide-ranging and often ill-defined terms of the debates over sprawl and Smart Growth, and both rely rather extensively on Randal O'Toole just to make sure

Atlanta, Georgia. Photograph by Digital-Vision.

there is a debate.[2] (Krieger especially seems to relish playing academic contrarian by giving the conservative O'Toole significant airtime but without rigorously analyzing his often-questionable statistics or claims.)[3] Both ask, "If sprawl is so terrible, why is it also so popular?" Krieger explores this question by focusing on the past and present historiography and on the battle for the public imagination. He emphasizes the need for political will in order to enact progressive policies but is skeptical that they can be realized. Kiefer asks pragmatic questions about the costs of redevelopment versus new development, about the real causes and cures of the problems, and what precisely distinguishes sprawl from smarter growth (not as simple a question as it may seem). If Krieger focuses on the role of policy to advance Smart Growth, Kiefer focuses on the need for Smart Growth alternatives to prove themselves to be more successful than sprawl in the marketplace.

The brief history of Smart Growth in Atlanta confirms that Krieger and Kiefer are both right. A crisis generated the political will to institute regional planning (even if it is not yet as effective as it might be), while recognition of the growing market for more urban living generated the popular will to support a growing number of mixed-use, higher density, and often transit-oriented developments (even if they are not as progressive as they might be).

Recognizing that no-growth policies were out of the question in booming Atlanta in 1995, the Georgia Conservancy, an environmental advocacy organization, partnered with the Atlanta chapters of the Urban Land Institute and the National Home Builders Association to host a series of symposia on combining environmental preservation with community planning.[4] Metro Atlanta's failure to meet ozone standards since 1978 was not at that time the principal focus of many of those concerned with the region's growth. However, it quickly became the sword of Damocles that transformed discussions of Smart Growth into actions. In 1996 the Environmental Protection Agency (EPA) warned Metro Atlanta that it would use its powers under Clean Air Act amendments to block future federal funding for highway construction unless the region took significant steps to reduce high ozone and smog levels. Despite attempts by the Atlanta Regional Commission (ARC) to produce an acceptable transportation plan intended to bring the region's air quality into compliance with state standards by 2005, in 1998 the region lost $700 million in federal transportation funds.[5]

When this loss was followed by a front-page story in the *Wall Street Journal* proposing that Atlanta's problems with sprawl might surpass those of Los Angeles and rumors that major companies had already decided against relocating to the region, top business leaders and government officials convened a series of "summit" meetings that led to the creation in 1999 of the Georgia Regional Transportation Authority (GRTA).[6] GRTA was charged with coordinating the planning and funding of transportation through the region. And while not specifically charged with connecting transportation and air quality to land use, GRTA leaders made this part of their mission in 2000 so that they could leverage transportation funding to steer local planning in accordance with the ARC's ten-county Regional Development Plan. That plan generally promotes Smart Growth development around existing activity centers and proposed transit stops and protection of watersheds but otherwise lacks regulatory power or more specific locational criteria for targeting where growth should and should not occur. However, regional planning was given further leverage in 2001 with the creation for a sixteen-county area of another regional planning agency, the Metropolitan North Georgia Water Planning District.[7] More recent regional initiatives have formed, focusing on open space acquisition, the arts, homelessness, governance, and interdisciplinary research and planning. All these coalitions are too new to have yet lived up to their potentials, let alone to have coordinated their planning with each other, but they have already fostered significant recognition of common agendas.[8]

In July 2000, the EPA eased its restrictions on federal transportation funds based on GRTA's agreement to enforce ARC's 1999 25-Year Transportation Plan, designating approximately $40 billion toward over two thousand transportation projects and programs intended to increase mobility and reduce harmful emissions, including major transit projects, bicycle paths, and sidewalks. Meanwhile another lawsuit is holding up $400 million worth of transportation funding, the EPA has further extended the Metro Atlanta deadline for air quality attainment to 2004, and the new governor just cut state funding from all but bus-related transit projects.

Despite these significant setbacks, acceptance of the value of regional planning and Smart Growth objectives has grown tremendously. In the late 1990s, several influential developers, most notably John Williams, CEO of Post Properties, one of the largest REITs in the country, and chair of the Metro Chamber of Commerce, committed themselves to New Urbanism and Smart Growth with in-town, urban, mixed-use projects.[9] Williams endowed a professorship at Georgia Tech to direct a new research Center for Quality Growth and Regional Development. In 1997, the Midtown Alliance, joining residents and business owners, began a community-based planning process that has resulted in a coherent urban vision of pedestrian-friendly streets; creation of a Midtown Improvement District that is planning $41 million in sidewalks, streetlights, and street trees; the largest rezoning in Atlanta's history; a Transportation Management Association; and a valuable model of redevelopment and urban living for other areas in the region. Over the past four years, the ARC's Livable Centers Initiative (LCI) has seeded revitalization planning for over forty projects in the region. This year the ARC began distributing implementation funds for the best LCI plans, most of them providing infrastructure to attract redevelopment of dead malls, vacant transit stops, or blighted commercial strips into mixed-use, pedestrian-friendly destinations.[10] This past year also saw the first express bus service between Atlanta and several suburban counties, three new live-work, mixed-use, and multifamily zoning ordinances in the city of Atlanta, a mixed-use redevelopment zoning overlay in Gwinnett County, approval of the first Transfer of Development Rights ordinance in the state (to preserve 40,000 of 60,000 acres in south Fulton County by directing growth to three new high-density urban villages), completion of over five thousand new residential units (mostly multifamily) in Midtown since 1997,[11] and construction on two particularly large transit-oriented redevelopments, Atlantic Station and Lindbergh City Center. Much of the credit for public interest and understanding of these initiatives goes to the excellent coverage since 1997 of development issues in the weekly "Horizon" section of the *Atlanta Journal-Constitution*.[12]

Thirty acres of underground parking garage were built at Atlantic Station, an example of Smart Growth and New Urbanism that far exceeds Krieger's concern that such projects are often simply prettily dressed-up suburbs in townlike iconography. Across a major highway from Atlanta's Midtown neighborhood and adjacent to Atlanta's Amtrak station, Atlantic Station is billed as the largest brownfield redevelopment project in the country. Construction of its two levels of parking and one level of building services is almost complete, and a dozen floors of the first office tower have been poured. The garage is simultaneously the containment cap over the contaminated soil from the site's former life as the Atlantic Steel Mill and the base for eight million square feet of retail, entertainment, office, hotel, and residential development. The rest of the 140-acre site calls for substantial amounts of housing, as well as lined, big-box retail, all aspiring for LEED energy-efficiency certification. As a model of Smart Growth, the $2-billion project was able to receive substantial public subsidies, including $38 million for a major bridge to Midtown, by convincing the EPA that the project's compactness and mixed uses would reduce vehicle trips enough to mitigate the region's poor air quality, thereby allowing it to bypass EPA's freeze on federal transportation funds and earn EPA's first Project XL designation, for excellence in public health and environmental protection cost effectiveness given to a real estate project. Several firms participated in the urban design, including TVS Architects of Atlanta and Duany Plater-Zyberk of Miami.

Krieger's article concludes with the discerning assertion that the benefits of sprawl tend to accrue to Americans individually, while the costs tend to be borne by society as a whole. This is certainly a perception most Atlantans have long shared. The region's explosive growth during the 1990s is largely attributed to the ease with which employers were able to attract in-migration due to the area's vaunted "quality of life."[13] From McMansions on "green-breasted lawns"[14] in Buckhead and Alpharetta to endless new, amenity-laden suburban and exurban houses and apartments on lush lots with access to good schools, new malls, and swank office parks, Atlanta has a particularly large supply of amenity-rich, upscale versions of the American Dream embedded within pompously named developments complete with country clubs and implied or functioning gated entries. This private version of The Good Life and its cheaper variants were built according to conventional auto-dependent, low-density suburban planning with separated uses and limited connectivity, contributing to all the usual regional-scale problems associated with sprawl. If the public problems of sprawl began to interfere with an individual's good life, the answer was simply to outrun it.

This worked for quite a while and propelled the Atlanta metropolitan area to its current twenty-nine-county area, over 100 miles in diameter. However, as commutes lengthened, Atlantans' driving increased. In 1999 they drove an average of thirty-five miles per person per day, the highest average daily vehicle-miles-traveled (VMT) in the United States.[15] Despite the fact that the highway system grew 16 percent faster than the population between 1982 and 1996 (and counter to the conclusions of the study cited by O'Toole), congestion has continued to rise, especially on the suburban arterials.[16] By 2000, Atlantans were spending fifty-three hours in traffic per year, up from twenty-five hours at the beginning of the 1990s, the fastest increase of any metro area.[17] Atlantans widely recognize this cost, and in what is sometimes called "the Atlanta effect," it is credited with helping lead the revival of interest in in-town living and working.

Other significant if far less recognized personal costs of sprawl are mounting. In 1998, the average metro Atlanta household spent 21.7 percent of its monthly income on transportation, second only to Houston's 22 percent and, surprisingly, more than the 19.6 percent they spent on shelter.[18] When I have shared these statistics with local friends or citizen groups, the numbers invariably produce an initial reaction of disbelief followed by nodding comprehension. Suddenly the big house on the big lot with the big car(s) and the big commute may not seem such a bargain, nor do the smaller in-town houses and condos in walkable, mixed-use neighborhoods close to transit seem quite so overpriced.

Similarly underrecognized are the costs to personal health associated with sprawl's heavy reliance on cars. Some of these are direct. In 1998, Atlanta had the highest automobile rider and pedestrian fatality rates of any major U.S. city.[19] Suburban teenagers with increasingly powerful vehicles are particularly accident-prone. The relative dearth of sidewalks on suburban roads may be partly to blame for the high pedestrian fatality rate. It is also cited by public health officials as one of the factors contributing to the higher rates of obesity associated with sprawl neighborhoods than urban neighborhoods.[20] Twenty-three percent of the Atlanta population (25 percent of fourth graders) is obese.[21] Public health researchers are increasingly studying the related health impacts of different physical environments, sedentary lifestyles, and long commutes.[22]

If the costs of sprawl to individuals tend to go unnoticed, so do the benefits to individuals of Smart Growth. Both Kiefer and Krieger cite the many arguments about the collective environmental, aesthetic, sociological, and economic benefits of Smart Growth but conclude that it will not be successful until it is more in the short-term self-interest of individuals and the market. They also both reference concern that the only self-interests that Smart Growth serve are those of existing elitist suburbanites trying to stop anyone else from enjoying their lifestyle and further exacerbating the traffic, overcrowded schools, and loss of open space. The curious aspect of this rather common critique is that, at least in Atlanta, there is little evidence of this constituency among the Smart Growth allies.[23] Quite the opposite. The newest suburban homeowners, often those trying to outrun sprawl by leapfrogging to the exurban fringe, are in fact the most likely to take a no-growth stance and raise vehement opposition to Smart Growth policies and higher density, mixed-use New Urbanist developments. Hall County, about sixty miles north of the city of Atlanta and currently the third fastest-growing county in the nation, voted to try to slow development, not by adopting Smart Growth strategies but by trying to slow growth and decrease density by increasing the minimum residential lot size from 25,000 to 35,000 square feet.[24]

The primary beneficiaries of Smart Growth in Atlanta have not been the self-protective existing suburbanites but the consumers who now have considerably more (and more attractive) choices of where to live and work. The changes have been most dramatic in town. They are evident in the rebuilt public housing projects at Centennial Place and Eastlake, the several new high-rise office and condo towers and the numerous "faux lofts" (since most of the old warehouses have already been converted), Technology Square (the mixed-use, urban expansion of Georgia Tech), and the countless new restaurants, cafés, and revitalized neighborhood centers. The new residents reversed the city of Atlanta's population decline, and whether they have been attracted by the urbanity of the new projects or the shortness of their commutes, their numbers are continuing to grow steadily.[25] Despite the economic downturn, urban development, in Midtown especially, has done well, if not thrived, and has revealed an eager market of consumers delighted to be offered more urban versions of the American Dream. The near doubling in aggregate property values in five years in Midtown and less dramatically in other in-town neighborhoods is raising concerns about gentrification (with many poorer residents being forced out to declining first-ring suburbs). But, as Kiefer suggests, it is also further legitimizing the value of well-designed urban redevelopment following Smart Growth principles.

There have also been increasing efforts to expand Smart Growth projects into the suburbs. The twin fourteen-story office towers of Phase I of Lindbergh City Center's grayfield retrofit of forty-seven acres along an in-town suburban strip are complete. An existing suburban MARTA rapid rail stop's parking lot is being redeveloped into several urban blocks with continuous ground-floor retail and five-story building heights fronting a Main Street and lining the taller commercial and residential towers. Master planned by Cooper Carry Architects in Atlanta, the development has found a primary tenant in BellSouth, Atlanta's second largest employer. BellSouth's decision in 1999 to consolidate 13,000 employees from seventy-five offices throughout Atlanta into three complexes at MARTA stops made headlines as an example of both good business (a high-tech company choosing urban locations to improve employee retention while also achieving the benefits of consolidation) and transit-oriented Smart Growth.[26]

Despite evidence of a suburban market for walkable, compact, mixed-use communities,[27] developers have been reluctant to undertake or unsuccessful at delivering more suburban greenfield New Urbanist mixed-use projects like New Manchester and Ridenour. These projects and efforts to incorporate housing into existing suburban office parks have met substantial opposition from communities and obstacles to financing.[28] Eventually, Ridenour may get a commuter rail stop on a proposed line and completion of office buildings as planned, better connecting it to the region. New Manchester, designed by Peter Calthorpe, connects its open space to a state park, expanding the benefits of both. These are key efforts to link these two projects to larger regional systems while also accomplishing Smart Growth goals within their boundaries. However, they remain relatively isolated islands of compact planning and preserved open space in the midst of conventionally zoned landscapes. To return to Kiefer's question about distinguishing sprawl and Smart Growth at a regional scale: are these the nodes of a pattern of healthy polynucleated growth or just aberrant reconfigured clusters of as-right development with minimal impact on the overall pattern? The difficulty of assessing whether a greenfield project is smart "enough" is fundamentally a question of whether it only serves its immediate inhabitants or serves the larger region. In other words, without a more developed regional plan to show how a single development, no matter how noble its intentions, significantly connects its roads, buildings, and open space to larger transportation, economic, and environmental systems, can we really determine how smart or sprawling such growth is?

These questions, and the example of Atlanta, reveal the messiness of Smart Growth in practice and what a long way we have to go to understand, let alone balance, all of the costs and benefits of sprawl and Smart Growth. The books reviewed by Krieger and Kiefer are a start and reflect the same kind of interdisciplinary conversations that have characterized Smart Growth discussion in Atlanta, but there is considerable need for continued design and research. Design visions of Smart Growth at all its scales and in all its varieties, from the region to the neighborhood to the building, and from the urban to the sub-urban, are essential tools in helping build the popular will to support political action for growth that happens by choice, not by chance. Similarly, continued research is needed into the complex interactions between design, density, transportation, public health, environmental sustainability, demographics, behavior, economic feasibility, law, and implementation. Unfortunately, our most reliable research methods have tended to be limited to questions of the narrowest scope. Designers' skills at synthesizing multiple agendas need to be brought into collaboration with research analysis, performance modeling, and policy making. Ultimately, Smart Growth's greatest impact may not be in its immediate consequences for the built environment but rather in breaking down the academic and professional barriers of specialization that have helped to produce our current landscape.

2004

Notes

1. Georgia Tech professor Steve French's urban design students studied alternative scenarios and found that even if the next million households in Atlanta locate only at existing activity centers, along existing corridors, or within an

Urban Growth Boundary and try to maximize ecological sustainability, several performance criteria would marginally improve, but the overall (sprawl) pattern established by the existing four million households would not significantly change. *Alternative Land Use Futures, Metropolitan Atlanta 2025,* Report from "Regional Land Use Studio," City and Regional Planning Program, College of Architecture, Georgia Institute of Technology, Fall 2002.

2. The debate may be becoming a battle. In the April/May 2003 issue of the *New Urban News,* a far from neutral voice in the debate, Philip Langdon's "The Right Attacks Smart Growth and New Urbanism" reports that a conference O'Toole convened in February 2003 on "Preserving the American Dream of Mobility and Homeownership" was principally devoted to laying the groundwork for a campaign aimed at stopping Smart Growth. He quotes David Strom of the Taxpayers League of Minnesota, "We often make the mistake of assuming this is a battle over who has the better facts." Langdon goes on to write, "Quite the contrary, he explained, policies aimed at shaping development are more likely to be defeated if voters get the impression that the typical smart growth leader is 'a pointy-headed intellectual fascist' trying to ruin people's lives." Adding further confusion to the debate, Duany spoke at the conference and emphasized the common interest between New Urbanism and the libertarians in free markets while de-emphasizing the common interest between New Urbanism and Smart Growth in linked urban and environmental regulation.

3. For a response to O'Toole's (and other's) critiques of Portland's problems with affordable housing, see Arthur C. Nelson, Rolf Pendall, Casey J. Dawkins, and Gerrit J. Knapp, "The Link between Growth Management and Housing Affordability: The Academic Evidence," Discussion Paper, Brookings Institution Center on Urban and Metropolitan Policy, February 2002. In addition to presenting considerable evidence that market demand, not land constraints, has been the primary determinant of housing prices in Portland and elsewhere, the authors point out that lower-middle- and lower-income families are more often priced out of areas that *lack* any growth management measures.

4. This strategy of shifting environmentalist opposition to growth to support for targeted growth linked to targeted conservation paralleled EPA's Smart Growth efforts at the time and similar coordination with HUD and DOT. The breadth of interdisciplinary collaboration achieved in the Georgia Conservancy's Smart Growth–oriented symposia, called Blueprints for Successful Communities, is reflected in the partners added since 1995: the AIA, ASLA, Atlanta Neighborhood Development Partnership, Georgia Trust for Historic Preservation, Georgia Planning Association, Institute of Transportation Engineers, the Consulting Engineers Council, and the National Association of Industrial and Office Properties. According to the Georgia Conservancy's Web site (www.gaconservancy.org), over four thousand people have

attended the symposia, on topics from transportation alternatives to state-wide planning for water.

5. The state environmental protection division rejected aspects of the plan, and a group of environmentalists successfully sued EPA's acceptance of "grandfathered" projects.

6. The Metro Atlanta Chamber of Commerce forwarded its Metropolitan Atlanta Transportation Initiative to then Governor-elect Roy Barnes in 1998. Its recommendations were incorporated into the governor's 1999 legislation creating GRTA.

7. In addition to problems with air quality, Atlanta's growth has contributed to problems with water quality and quantity. The Atlanta region relies on surface water for 98 percent of its needs, 80 percent of which comes from the basin of the Chattahoochee River, one of the smallest rivers to supply a major metropolitan area in the United States. It is predicted to be the first East Coast city to engage in West Coast–style water wars. See the North Georgia Water Management Web site, www.northgeorgiawater.com, and Douglas Jehl, "Atlanta's Growing Thirst Creates Water War," *New York Times,* May 27, 2002, A1–9.

8. In addition to the single-issue, regionally focused initiatives described above, several Atlanta-based, interdisciplinary groups have formed to address the interconnectedness of growth-related issues: Sustainable Atlanta Roundtable, the Smart Growth Partnership, the Georgia Quality Growth partnership, and the already mentioned Blueprints for Successful Communities.

9. In Atlanta, "in-town" refers to the several municipalities and neighborhoods within the thirty-five-mile circumference Perimeter Highway, Interstate 285. Approximately half of this area is occupied by the city of Atlanta and its three most developed neighborhoods: Downtown, Midtown, and Buckhead. Much of in-town's character is suburban, but it is generally perceived to be more urban than the suburbs beyond the Perimeter Highway in the now twenty-nine-county area that constitutes metro Atlanta.

10. Recognizing the potential role of livable, mixed-use development associated with transit to improve regional transportation (and air quality), the ARC, in its 1999 25-Year Regional Transportation Plan, approved $1 million per year for five years for the LCI grants program and $350 million for implementation. The grants provide funding to local communities for redevelopment plans that are mixed-use, enhance streetscaping and sidewalks, emphasize the pedestrian, improve access to transit and other transportation options, and expand housing opportunities. Twenty-five communities will receive a total of $27 million in federal transportation funds for implementation this year. Communities must match 20 percent of the funds. See www.atlantaregional.org/qualitygrowth/lci, and Janet Frankston, "ARC Ready to Bestow Grants," *Atlanta Journal-Constitution,* May 19, 2003, E1.

11. This significantly surpasses the goal of four thousand new residential

units by the year 2017 set by Midtown Alliance, a powerful neighborhood civic group, during its Blueprint Midtown planning process in 1997. *Midtown Journal,* Spring 2003.

12. Journalist David Goldberg's development of and writing for the "Horizon" section has achieved statewide and national recognition. In 1999 when the Georgia State Legislature created GRTA, it also passed a resolution commending his leadership, and the Radio-Television News Directors Association and Foundation invited him to write *Covering Urban Sprawl: Rethinking the American Dream; An RTNDF Journalist's Resource Guide,* available at www.rtnda.org.

13. In 2002 Atlanta surpassed Chicago as home to the third largest collection of Fortune 500 companies; Russell Grantham, "Atlanta Now No. 3 as Headquarters City," *Atlanta Journal-Constitution,* April 2, 2002, C1. Lawrence D. Frank, Kevin Green, David Goldberg, Gregg Logan, and Todd Noel report that between 1990 and 2000 the Atlanta region added 671,700 net new jobs, leading the nation in job creation, and led all U.S. housing markets with a total of 457,557 new housing units; "Trends, Implications and Strategies for Balanced Growth in the Atlanta Region," The SMARTRAQ research program at the Georgia Institute of Technology, 2002. Census data reveal that those homes are larger than the national average. "The average Georgia 'housing unit' grew from 5.52 rooms in 1990 to 6.24 rooms in 2000—a 13 percent jump. Metro Atlanta averages 6.27 rooms, significantly higher than the national average of 5.3 rooms." Marlon Manuel, "Built with Rooms to Grow: Metro Area Homes Bigger," *Atlanta Journal-Constitution,* September 21, 2002, A1.

14. A phrase from Tom Wolfe's fictional but insightful description of the residential landscape in Buckhead, one of Atlanta's more upscale neighborhoods. *A Man in Full* (New York: Farrar, Straus & Giroux, 1998).

15. Texas Transportation Institute, *Urban Mobility Study: 2000* (College Station, TX: November 2000).

16. "Over the 15 years from 1982 through 1996, the period covered by the report, Atlanta built more new lanes on its freeways and arterial roads than all but the nation's three largest metro areas. Atlanta was one of the few places whose highway system grew at a faster rate than its population: 69 percent vs. 53 percent. The region now has more miles of freeway lanes per 1,000 residents than any place but Dallas, Texas"; David Goldberg, "Study Certifies It: Atlanta Traffic Stinks," *Atlanta Journal* and *Atlanta Constitution,* November 18, 1998, A1, referring to the Texas Transportation Institute's annual report on urban mobility.

17. Kelly Simmons, "Atlanta Tailgating L.A. on Gridlock," *Atlanta Journal-Constitution,* May 8, 2001, A1, referring to the Texas Transportation Institute's annual report on urban mobility.

18. The average American household spent 18 percent of its income on

transportation in 1998, but the figure rose 8 percent between 1990 and 1998 and is likely to have continued to rise at this rate. In 1998 Bostonians spent 15.2 percent of their income on transportation and 24.6 percent on shelter. Charles Longer, Tom Lalley, Barbara McCann, "Driven to Spend: The Impact of Sprawl on Household Transportation Expenses," *Surface Transportation Policy Project Report,* November 2000, www.transact.org.

19. National Highway Traffic Safety Administration, 1999, as quoted in Richard Jackson, "Rebuilding the Unity of Health and the Environment," in H. Frumkin, R. Jackson, and C. Coussens, eds., *Health and the Environment in the Southeastern United States* (Washington, DC: National Academies Press, 2002).

20. Richard J. Jackson and Chris Kochtitzky, "Creating a Healthy Environment: The Impact of the Built Environment on Public Health," Sprawl Watch Clearinghouse Monograph Series, November 2001.

21. Elizabeth Lee, "37% of Children in Georgia Tip the Scales Too Far," *Atlanta Journal-Constitution,* May 16, 2003, A1.

22. It is not a coincidence that one of the leading researchers in this field lives in Atlanta. Dr. Richard Jackson, the director of the National Center for Environmental Health at the Centers for Disease Control and Prevention, had an epiphany regarding the unrecognized but substantial impact of the physical design of the environment on mortality in a region with a burgeoning immigrant population, no sidewalks, and one of the highest pedestrian kill rates in the country. While stuck in traffic on Buford Highway, a suburban arterial, Jackson saw a pedestrian struggling in the heat and realized that if she died, the cause of death would simply read heat stroke, not poor urban design, no crosswalks, sidewalks, or shade trees, and unreliable bus service.

23. It is easy to take potshots at suburban environmentalists driving SUVs with Sierra Club bumper stickers and concoct conspiracy theories. But it is important to distinguish the no-growthers from the Smart Growthers. In Atlanta, the Georgia Conservancy is an important advocate for regional planning, transit-oriented development, suburban redevelopment, and other Smart Growth strategies that the organization believes will help improve air and water quality in the region.

24. Janet Frankston, "Hall Votes to Increase Minimum Lot Sizes," *Atlanta Journal-Constitution,* May 9, 2003, C3.

25. U.S. Bureau of Census's latest statistics are for 2000 to 2001 and show Atlanta receiving an average of 502 new residents every day, the fifth highest in the country. Of those, 83 a day chose to live in the city of Atlanta. Julie B. Hairston, Maurice Tamman, "502 Move In Daily," *Atlanta Journal-Constitution,* May 21, 2003, B1. This is a rapid increase. From April 1998 to April 1999, the city only grew by 900 residents, or an average of less than 3 per day. David Firestone, "Suburban Comforts Thwart Atlanta's Plans to Limit Sprawl," *New York Times,* November 21, 1999.

26. See Matt Grove, "BellSouth Plan Tackles Transportation Troubles," *Atlanta Business Chronicle*, March 6, 2000; and David Goldberg, *BellSouth's Atlanta Metro Plan: A Case Study in Employer-Driven Smart Growth*, Sprawl Watch Clearinghouse Report, www.sprawlwatch.org.

27. Based on soon-to-be-published data collected for a Personal Preference and Behavior Survey of eight hundred Atlanta households, by Dr. Lawrence Frank's SMARTRAQ research project at the Georgia Institute of Technology.

28. The cost of structured parking, even when shared between commercial and residential, tends to raise rents beyond competitive rates in the suburbs, where land is cheap and surface parking is the norm. This contributes both to the decentralization of Atlanta's office market and the difficulties of building more compact developments in the suburbs. Only 11.33 percent of Atlanta's metro employment is within three miles of the Central Business District, while 61.9 percent is outside a ten-mile ring. Edward L. Glaeser, Matthew Kuhn, and Chenghuan Chu, "Job Sprawl: Employment Location in U.D. Metropolitan Areas," Brookings Institution, Survey Series, May 2001.

7

Diversity by Law:
On Inclusionary Zoning
and Housing

Jerold S. Kayden

At a time when the real estate market has made it increasingly difficult for American cities to foster or maintain social and economic diversity, "diversity by law" zoning programs are attracting new attention. Using such labels as "inclusionary zoning" and "inclusionary housing," some local governments—including those in Cambridge, Massachusetts; Montgomery County, Maryland; and Santa Fe, New Mexico—are mandating that private developers provide low-income housing along with their market-rate units as a condition for project approval. Developers might be required to construct the affordable units on-site, or arrange to have them constructed off-site, or make an "in lieu of construction" cash contribution to a government-established housing trust fund. The developer's obligation might range from 10 to 25 percent of the units of a project, and the developer might be allowed to build additional market-rate units to mitigate the financial burden.

Inclusionary zoning stands in stark contrast to the dominant, albeit de facto, U.S. practice of exclusionary zoning. For half a century, suburban governments have enlisted zoning ordinances as foot soldiers in the battle against housing for lower-income people and racial and ethnic minorities. The weapons are varied. Some ordinances preclude the construction of multifamily housing. Some dictate superficially benign requirements—such as lot and unit minimum sizes—that can make housing unaffordable for many. The effect of such provisions has been considerable, especially for inner-city residents who might wish to move to the suburbs were affordable housing available.

Although the rules that govern what local governments do with their zoning ordinances issue from state legislatures, such legislatures have been reluctant to interfere with exclusionary local practices. Even attempts such as Massachusetts's "anti-snob" zoning act, which provides an accelerated, comprehensive review process for low- and moderate-income housing development applications, have failed to deter local exclusion. And the federal government, other than passing anti-discrimination laws to combat racial discrimination in rental housing, has also stayed on the sidelines. Not surprisingly, the only significant initiative to tackle local exclusion has come from the judiciary—the branch of government most insulated from the intensity of majority displeasure. As recounted by Charles Haar in *Suburbs under Siege: Race, Space, and Audacious Judges* and by David Kirp in *Our Town: Race, Housing, and the Soul of Suburbia,* the New Jersey Supreme Court required local governments to open the door to affordable housing by effecting a judicial takeover of local zoning insofar as it controlled the development of low- and moderate-income housing.

What accounts, then, for the new look into inclusionary policies? Interest in housing diversity springs from both selfless and selfish concerns. In some communities, older residents have found that their adult children cannot afford to buy a home in the towns where they were raised. In others, citizens have realized that lower-paying service jobs in public and private sectors are difficult to fill when potential employees cannot afford to live in the community and must commute. Some places have discovered that their cultural life suffers from lack of demographic and income diversity. And some individuals have concluded that the social contract that ideally bonds Americans of different classes is weakened when one group is isolated by geography from the opportunities enjoyed by the others.

Ironically, even were the political will mustered, the adoption of inclusionary laws would face their severest challenge from the judiciary—the branch that has (as noted above) levied the only serious public challenge to exclusionary zoning. This challenge owes to the fact that private housing developers often resist being required to help solve a problem—the scarcity of affordable housing—that they did not create; they argue that the burden should be more widely distributed, perhaps in the form of government subsidies for affordable housing.

The Fifth Amendment to the U.S. Constitution states, "nor shall private property be taken for public use, without just compensation"; thus, government laws may not deny property owners all economically viable uses of their property. In *Nollan v. California Coastal Commission* and *Dolan v. City of Tigard,* the U.S. Supreme Court ruled that the Constitution demands careful scrutiny of conditions placed on land-use development to assure that such conditions are related to an identifiable public interest endangered by the proposed development. For example, if a proposed housing subdivision would demonstrably generate additional and burdensome traffic, then a local government would be allowed to condition its approval on an agreement that the developer expand, at his or her own expense, a right-of-way for the new traffic. But a local government would be overstepping its authority if it required that the developer fund construction of an eight-lane expressway—a road that would serve a population far larger than the residents of the new subdivision.

The challenge for a community that wishes to adopt inclusionary programs is to show not only that additional market-rate housing would harm its interests, but also that these harmful effects would be mitigated by inclusionary requirements. In meeting this challenge, the very idea of diversity and its benefits is critical.

Just as proponents of affirmative action argue that such policies benefit not only minorities but also majorities, by expanding their contact with previously unfamiliar social, economic, and cultural realities, so too many proponents of housing diversity argue that their communities would benefit from wider representations of society. To be sure, that argument will not convince every suburban resident, especially those who have moved to suburbia precisely to avoid contact with diverse groups. But the diversity argument may resonate with developers with inclusionary obligations. When communities muster the political will to enact inclusionary policies—even if the communities are liberal strongholds such as Cambridge and Santa Fe—then those developers who construct market-rate housing exclusively may be promoting homogeneity detrimental to a freely chosen public good.

1999

8

The Spectacle
of Ordinary Building

Mitchell Schwarzer

In *The Society of the Spectacle,* Guy Debord defined the world of the
spectacle as corresponding to that "moment when the commodity
has attained the total occupation of social life." In the decades since
Debord's 1967 manifesto, the commodity—the central feature of the
marketplace system in which needs and desires are channeled through
purchases—has come nearly to dominate the built landscape of the
United States. Today the weight of relentless consumption lies heavy
on ordinary architecture, from single-family houses to big-box stores
to office parks.

Buildings are a special type of commodity. Like other products, they
are bought and sold, advertised and merchandised within the consumer
marketplace. Buildings and landscapes also serve as the dominant settings for commodity manufacture, display, exchange, and use. This
dual role has important implications for the ways in which buildings
signify. Buildings must refer to themselves, but more crucially, they
must provide space and surface for the significatory practices of mobile
commodities.

From a historical point of view, what is happening now is not new.
The spectacle of the commodity was evident in the great world exposi-
tions and fairs of the second half of the nineteenth century. During the
Gilded Age, the Roaring Twenties, and the long postwar prosperity,

74

ordinary buildings and landscapes were key aspects of a commodity aesthetic, a regime of visual understanding coincident with economic exchange.

Yet a close inspection of the built landscape of the past quarter century reveals new and higher levels of building commodification. Ordinary buildings are increasingly tied to a ruthlessly competitive system of consumption. On the one hand, their design is driven by market research and financially rationalized construction processes; as a result, buildings are cheaper, larger, and more comfortable and convenient. On the other hand, their function is coordinated with ever-greater numbers of products and signs; the ordinary environment is, in all sorts of new ways, filled with the shrill messages of the media and advertising industries. Never before could one travel such vast distances—from Houston to Salt Lake City, from the edge cities of Washington to the ever-spreading sprawl of Los Angeles—and experience built environments of such relentless efficiency and generic sameness.

The recent built landscape cannot be understood without a recognition of the waning influence of the architectural profession. Since the early 1970s, the schisms of postmodernity have been unraveling the project of architectural modernism, exposing the inadequacies of its rhetoric of functional design and utopian urbanism. Paralleling the American culture at large, the building industry ignores high architectural ideas, especially those distanced from commodity aesthetics. Nowadays, most architects must cater to buyers, marketers, and building specialists, whose overlapping spheres of influence erode the profession's standing.

Meanwhile, the metaphors and the mystique of technology have changed radically. The digital revolution has relegated the parallelism between architecture and the machine to the antique past. Le Corbusier's dictum "the house is a machine for living in" might now be restated "the landscape is a central processing unit for selling lavish living." This landscape is driven equally by electronic seductions for immediate gratification and by boundless choice.

How has all this come about? How has ever-accelerating consumption produced a standardized environment characterized by an ever-widening gap between products and their containers? And what architectural strategies might relieve this new bleakness, this white-noise geography of places where low-wage workers set the table for our feast of consumption?

Architecture, Technology, and the New Economy

Capital markets have long played the leading role in shaping the built environment, but in previous eras their role was tempered by the architectural, planning, and engineering disciplines. From the nineteenth century until the 1960s, the market-driven construction of buildings and landscapes was often enhanced, even elevated, by technological inventions and paradigm-shifting architectural ideas. I am thinking, for instance, of the marvelous ingenuity with which buildings were made to accommodate the elevator, steel and reinforced concrete frames, plate glass, and fluorescent lighting; one result of these inventions was the skyscraper. Architectural and planning movements too developed important and influential ideas. The Arts and Crafts, City Beautiful, and Modern movements all introduced significant theories that probed the nature of facade, plan, function, and symbolism. The architecture of ordinary buildings during much of America's Industrial Age can be understood as vernacular translations made from these and other artistic movements. Consider the scores of Craftsman bungalows, Beaux Arts banks, and Modernist office buildings built between the 1880s and 1960s; in the United States, unlike in Europe, oppositional avant-gardes were not prominent. Rather, the power of architecture derived largely from its ability to help coordinate economic forces and, in the best of cases, to sculpt them into beautiful forms.

Much has changed. The priority of technological innovation is now pragmatic efficiency—minimizing the use of expensive materials, streamlining production, and achieving heightened levels of function as well as client satisfaction. Flimsy, artificial materials like DryVit and Exterior Insulation and Finish Systems encase much new construction and reduce assembly costs. Pouring concrete panels and tilting them up into place make cheap walls. New thermal glazing technologies run electric currents through glass to make windows work as walls, achieving greater climate control and comfort. Seismic standards can now be extended beyond minimum life-safety thresholds. Computer-Aided Drafting is now networked to business practices and client services; from the first keystroke, CAD helps determine choices not only for lines and compositions but also for specifications and materials, thus linking the processes of design and business.

Specialists, for instance, in structural or financial or environmental control systems, cross all aspects of design, making it harder for architects to innovate independently. In fact, to attract clients, many architects have become specialists in particular building types, elements, or procedures. Performance criteria for success discourage experiments with prototypes. As in the automobile industry, changes in building design and technology focus on refinement and marketing. Well-tested formulas guarantee results and meet expectations for revenues. Ordinary buildings are products that must be flexible and profitable—products, in the industry lingo, that are made to "flip."

Today, architectural movements are buried in the metaphors of the past, and buried too are the powers of those movements to push experimental ideas into everyday building culture. Aside from neo-traditional urbanism, no recent architectural movement has won even limited popular following. The concepts that once trickled down from the most thoughtful architecture toward ordinary building no longer do so. Postmodernism was the last architectural movement to achieve widespread recognition and influence. Too eagerly responsive to the mass marketplace, however, Postmodernism devolved into another form of spectacle.

To be sure, exciting and visionary architecture is still being built all across the country. New York and Los Angeles in particular have nurtured creative and theoretical architectural cultures, led by designers like Frank Gehry, Thom Mayne, Steven Holl, Tod Williams and Billie Tsien, and Peter Eisenman. But these scenes are small, and, more important, their impact on the landscape is inconsequential. Today's sought-after architects tend to be individual stars, designing high-profile projects as linchpins for cultural or leisure-time development schemes. Their works do not produce any real consensus among thoughtful architects, the kind of consensus that then might influence the broader building culture.

Dwelling Large

In *Modernity at Large,* Arjun Appadurai argues that ostentation is not necessarily the key quality of consumption but rather the quality we notice. "Even in the most fashion-ridden of contexts," he writes, "consumption leans toward habituation through repetition."[1] The effects of ostentatious and repetitious spectacle are evident almost everywhere. Much critical energy has been trained at McMansions, those pseudo palaces that trumpet affluence. But McMansions are not unusual in their excess. The latest data from the National Association of Home Builders tell us that ordinary single-family houses are getting bigger; average size has risen from 1,600 square feet in 1975 to more than 2,200 square feet today.

Big new houses contain big new volumes. Far beyond the private worlds described by Walter Benjamin in "Paris, Capital of the 19th Century," domestic interiors are now galaxies unto themselves. And the space of these galaxies is extended via screen images, from cable television to videos to personal computers. Thus, the organization of houses is connected to global image fields, wired via telephone lines, coaxial cables, and fiber optics. These wires hollow out social experiences, such as shopping, which once occurred mainly in public realms. As I write this essay at my desk in San Francisco, I watch UPS, FedEx, and Webvan trucks queue on my street, delivering goods ordered on the Internet. The lot lines of my neighborhood come to resemble the checkout lines of a store, heralding the phenomenon of live-shop buildings.

By any measure, new homes are bloated. Modernist architects once designed slender load-paths of steel or concrete to bring material forces down to earth; today contractors load material upward and outward. The recent vogue for three-car garages has already been superceded by the trend to four-car garages. Where else to store the cars, SUVs, boats, dirt bikes, kayaks, and other products that allow the American family to scratch the consumer itch? And since people need more storage space than ever, closets, shelves, and cabinets have grown in size and sophistication. (So too have the climate-controlled, carpeted warehouses where one can rent space to store yesterday's purchases or seasonal possessions. There are not enough landfills in which to bury the residue of consumption.)

In new homes, cathedral-ceilinged entries exaggerate the impression of bigness. So does the shift in programmatic priority from formal living and dining rooms to informal "big rooms," flexible areas for eating, socializing, and being entertained. Social conventions are not what they once were; formal rooms are a shrinking luxury, as media rooms, kitchens, closets, bedrooms, and bathrooms balloon. It is now commonplace to build a bathroom for every bedroom. Alongside personal televisions, phones, computers, and music systems, personal bathrooms mean that family members will never need to negotiate or argue over the use of things. The bulking up and technological wizardry of the home allow us to control rather than share our private worlds—a practice that only exacerbates the long-standing trend toward household disintegration described in 1956 by Max Weber: "With the multiplication of life chances and opportunities, the individual becomes less and less content with being bound to rigid and undifferentiated forms of life prescribed by the group."[2]

Indeed, for many contemporary Americans, community seems more an optional pleasure than a civic obligation. Privacy is prized in new developments. Windows that face onto the neighbor's house are avoided. So are side entrances that might lead to chance encounters. And the obsession with privacy is matched by the concern for safety. Security is paramount, and much effort is devoted to alarms, fences, and protective lighting and landscaping. No wonder gated communities are one of the fastest growing sectors of residential construction. Their roads, sidewalks, plantings, and driveways are superbly controlled means to private ends.

The urge for control and privacy begets sameness. In planned communities across the United States, consistency of image is the most important contributor to the sense of shared public space. The arbitrary-sounding names—Oak Glen, Oak Grove, Oak Gully—are astute rhetorical devices that associate one's particular community with other successfully packaged communities. Residential construction has entered the age of niche specialization, in which signage, landscaping, and building design all reinforce an image marketed to a particular group.

In general, choices for residential design are limited, their styling traditional and risk averse. In a subdivision of hundreds of houses, all might look much the same. Monotonous postwar developments like Levittown, New York, or Lakewood, California, were once unusual; they are now the norm. Unlike popular music, clothing, and movies, whose imagery is often enlivened by outsiders—for instance, bohemians, gangster rappers, outdoor fanatics, slackers—domestic architecture generally adheres to old-fashioned gentry values of good living. Most bare-bones homes and starter mansions replay the tried and true. Individual expression is applauded in consumer design but not in architecture—individuality must not undermine a development's familiarity, its buyers' loyalty, and its houses' utility for showcasing other commodities. (In fact, in super-hot real estate zones like the San Francisco Bay Area, the showcasing of commodities is used to sell houses. The decor of most homes, according to consultants, inhibits their selling for the highest possible price. To stimulate buyers, interiors are outfitted with rented furnishings—with designer lamps, kitchenware, rugs, and so on. And it is better if these trucked-in things look new and coordinated, rather like a Michael Graves display at Target or a feature in *Martha Stewart Living*.)

Animating Sales

Out on retail row, fierce competition spins out a dizzying array of stores and products. Over the past quarter century, retail buildings have become larger and more profitable. At the same time, larger inventories and calculated product displays are creating complex image environments. As described by David Ogilvy, the construction of brand image is the result of many factors—product nature, name, packaging, price, and advertising—working together to craft a visible and distinct personality.[3] But one powerful effect of thousands of competing product lines is to make retail buildings themselves recede into the background. The consumer's attention is not worth wasting on an appreciation of architecture.

Retail business goals for greater market share depend on increasing selection and reducing price. Such goals lead to larger buildings. Average supermarket dimensions have leaped from 10,000 square feet twenty-five years ago to 50,000 square feet today. Superstores reap greater profits by adding high-markup gourmet products and non-food items to traditional low-markup food items. Likewise, the size of malls defies any steady-state equilibrium. New super-regional malls contain three to four anchor stores, each with 100,000 or so square feet. The Mall of America, which opened in 1992, lords over seventy-eight acres in Bloomington, Minnesota; it is a vacation destination. In the middle of this 4.2-million-square-foot complex is a seven-acre theme park, Knott's Camp Snoopy. Outside are 4.5 million square feet of parking lots.

Lest we forget, value retail has been the trade darling of the past decade. It includes discounters (Wal-Mart, Target), category killers (Toys "R" Us, Circuit City, Pet-Mart, Barnes & Noble), warehouse clubs (Sam's Club, Price Club), and combinations of these (and other) types in power centers and value malls. The size of these big boxes is astounding. A new Ikea home furnishings store in Emeryville, California, measures 274,000 square feet. Power centers containing up to twelve big boxes crest at more than 1 million square feet. Image counts as much as size. The names of stores have been puffed up. Kmart did not sound big enough, so it became Big K. Target is now Target Greatland.

Strip centers, regional malls, and power centers establish a new kind of scale. In older areas, new retail squats awkwardly amid the finer grains of older buildings, presenting appallingly blank exterior walls. But in newer parts of the metropolis, retail's gargantuan dimensions mesh with the imperial scale of industrial parks, airports, and the interstate.

The postwar strip and its garish neon lights related directly to roadside perception. By contrast, most new popular retail is set off from arterial roads by gigantic parking lots with token plantings; shoppers appear as specks in this panorama. To provide environments where consumption is dominant, new shopping areas are self-contained, labyrinthine. I had a harder time negotiating the outlet mall at Woodbury Commons, New York, than the medieval medinas of Morocco; the complicated organization of buildings, roads, and parking lots forced me, against my usual habits, to drive between stores with a crumpled map in one hand. The plastic signs in these environments are simple

Abandoned Kmart. Photograph by Virgil Hancock III; courtesy of Etherton Gallery.

but colossal. Walls and floors are economical and interminable, football fields of Pirelli flooring. On the fronts of buildings, ornament might drip over an edge here and there, like a half-baked idea fleetingly catching our attention; ornamental language has been diluted, intended only to direct us to the main experience of consumption.

The latest retail lingo promotes entertainment experiences, moments in which the hunt for possessions resounds with adventure and rapture—albeit in calculated circumstances. In cities and suburbs, "shoppertainment" complexes sell leisure products along with movie tickets, dining, and other amusements like children's play spaces and displays of digital technology. Concept stores like Niketown and the Nature Company, concept environs like Caesar's Palace in Las Vegas and the Metreon in San Francisco, and concept districts like Times Square in New York and the Inner Harbor in Baltimore bundle sales with amusements and exhibitions that stamp memories for future shoppertainment experiences. "Leisure," as Jean Baudrillard wrote, "is not the availability of time, it is its display . . . this exhibition and over-exhibition of itself as such."[4]

In magnitude can be read the collective will, the appetites that repeat in individuals. Within the big boxes, clear-span spaces and warehouse-height ceilings pretend that there is no enclosure. Consumers lose themselves in a fantasy of plenitude, "the zombie effect" described by William Kowinski in *The Malling of America*.[5] Appearance is about packing lines of vision with catchy items, seductive slogans, and manipulations that induce people into buying things they had not thought about before. Contemporary retail researchers like Paco Underhill know about drawing customers beyond the "decompression zones" of visual disinterest (at store entrances, for instance) and about making use of such odd research findings as the fact that most people turn right once inside the mall; if perception of spatial limits is clouded and consciousness of time arrested, consumers might spend more time, penetrate deeper to "destination items," and of course spend more money.[6]

Labored Horizons

Places of work in America are likewise designed along lines straight and wide. In a reversal of earlier booms, when buildings created skylines, today's office buildings are not getting taller. The glamorous skyscraper—

Schaumburg, Illinois, 1995. Photograph copyright Bob Thall.

Bartlett, Illinois, 1993. Photograph copyright Bob Thall.

Itasca, Illinois, 1993. Photograph copyright Bob Thall.

the corporate icon—is now judged an unnecessary expense; mid-rise and low-rise complexes, which maximize rentable space and minimize service space, are more cost-effective. Data gathered by the Urban Land Institute show that whereas companies once settled for 20,000- to 25,000-square-foot floor plates, many now opt for 30,000- to 60,000-square-foot measurements. Business priorities for expansion and/or exit strategies encourage simple rectangular plans and inexpensive materials; they discourage extravagant architectural statements. Large low boxes are the currency of work environs—from the containers stacked at seaports to factories, warehouses, distribution centers, and convention centers. Their dimensions, like those of big-box stores, respond to market efficiencies as well as to the inchoate ambience of globalism.

Fitting new mega-boxes into existing cities is an art, but it is an art of space maximization and public relations. Despite global computer networks, huge trade shows at convention centers remain the best way to showcase products for distributors and buyers. Hence the trend toward increasing the size of these places. In the early 1980s, convention centers could manage with spaces well under 1 million square feet. Today, unless such centers are considering expansions to between 1.3 and 2 million square feet, they flirt with obsolescence. During the years I lived in Chicago in the early 1990s, and during all the years since, the city's McCormick Place Convention Center has been blanketed by the formwork and machinery of continuous expansion. Its exhibition space now contains 2.2 million square feet.

The successful work building, like the successful residence or store, effects a seamless continuum with markets. Many work buildings are no more than brief stops on an expansive conveyor belt intended to maximize the profits of all the enterprises it connects as it transports products from place to place, from purchase to purchase. Our relationship to commodities is characterized by an increased pace of exchange and movement, and by decreased time for use or reflection. As Paul Virilio has written, "The more speed grows, the more 'control' tends to supercede even the environment, the real time of interactivity replacing the real space of corporeal activity."[7]

Post-elite Design

In *Learning from Las Vegas,* Robert Venturi, Denise Scott Brown, and Steven Izenour analyzed the Las Vegas Strip and its contrast of fantastic signage and recessive buildings. The authors recognized that the capacity of signs to facilitate movement and communication distinguished them from the static buildings they fronted. Today, however, the "decorated shed" described in that influential book no longer compels us. A case in point is the evolution of the cinema from movie palace to multiplex. In the early and glory days of Hollywood, it mattered that theater buildings conveyed the mystery and glamour of the movie capital. Aristocratic, exotic, or futuristic decor was typical. Signs and marquees were landmarks. Contemporary multiplexes rarely aim to be architectural blockbusters; big ambitions are reserved for their changeable (and quickly dischargeable) contents. The surfaces and even the signage of the multiplex are subdued. The action is on the screen, in dark auditoriums where consumers are transported into worlds of special effects and wraparound sound.

Similarly, today's gasoline stations, roadside restaurants, and motor inns seem reluctant to convey much fantasy or fun. Few and far between are gas stations with pseudomodernist sheets of glass and thin exploding slabs of concrete. Gone are restaurants in the shape of donuts or parasols, and motels that evoke the South Seas or Wagon

Train. The increasingly chain-operated roadside is less kitschy, more no-nonsense. Themed environments abound elsewhere; on the road we find buildings that fit into standardized categories and bland but recognizable brand identities. One gets more services and pays higher rates, for instance, at a Comfort Inn than at a Sleep Inn, although both are owned by the same company and are similarly nondescript. Building development is becoming a p-word, the outcome of detailed analyses of place, product, price, promotion, politics, and public relations.

Thus, ordinary building has become the backdrop for the showtime of programmed distraction, a system for commerce, a sound stage for affluent lifestyle, a pragmatic infrastructure that sustains flights of individual desire. In its enabling function, the built landscape is extralarge, horizontal, orthogonal, and anonymous. New buildings are efficient and flexible, taciturn and interchangeable. They are like laboratory clones, alike in motive and geometry.

Because ordinary development facilitates the forces of mobile consumption, its architecture is overwhelmed by its contents, by its awesome variety of stuff, the off-the-scale promotions and displays. Media messages and commodities buffet rooms, corridors, and roads. On ubiquitous stages—for example, on screens and speakers, in glossy infomercials and pictorial blurbs—we can experience everything that is for sale in every conceivable psychological or pop-cultural packaging. Out on the thoroughfares, the view of the buildings is inundated by billboards, signs, video screens, as well as by the distractions of Palm Pilots and cell phones. Inside, our appreciation of surfaces and details is drowned out by the piped-in jingles and the shelves of products that express our culture's omnivorous materialism.

There is less and less need for ordinary buildings to look distinct or to provoke thought. Architectural structure, surface, and detail are no longer effective communicators of popular messages. These messages, influenced by fashion and dependent on digital technology, are too quick for the slow and lasting processes of building. Our eyes are conditioned by film, video, and computers to see objects in states of representation, dramatization, animation, and, of course, commodification. By comparison, most buildings appear lethargic, devoid of life. Popular messages are oriented more to disorderly mass or individual preferences than to the stratified societal relations that architecture so often served in the past—for instance, the distinctions of metropolitan and provincial, or spiritual and profane.

Will future architectural creativity, apart from matters of efficiency and comfort, be encouraged only by the increasingly few enlightened public, institutional, or business clients and by wealthy patrons? Or can architects respond in other ways to an American built landscape shaped by the spectacle of the commodity?

It is now hard to conceive of buildings as discrete creations of an architect. For too long, the profession has operated according to an outmoded Renaissance vision of design as orchestrated by the architect-creator. Adhering to this model will only marginalize further the contributions of the architectural profession. Trickle-down cultural movement is an outdated concept. As recent popular and artistic culture shows, design ideas and trends move in many directions. We live within an intricate matrix of cultural creation, based less on hierarchy or old aristocratic models than on the ironies of individual conformity, the romances of outsider insurgence, and the unchartable flows of global ideas. It is futile to hope that a coherent and unified architectural movement will emerge and once again give direction to ordinary building.

Nonetheless, there are many approaches architects can take. First, as in the past, public policy can and should significantly influence the built environment. Planning codes and regulations are the strongest tools we possess for reducing the effects of the commodity on landscapes and buildings. As the New Urbanists have shown, when architects take seriously the need to transmit their ideas through legal codes, the landscape can be shaped by ideas that transcend values of the bottom line. Why shouldn't other architects with different ideas about the built environment successfully follow the pragmatic model of the New Urbanists? There is great potential for architects and city planners to collaborate on writing design principles, scenarios that appeal to the diverse desires of American consumers now untapped by the real estate industry. Government-sponsored design codes need not look to the past or be authoritarian—citizens might even participate in their ad hoc creation.

And there are other ways of organizing built space besides governmental codes. Architects like Diller/Scofidio and Rem Koolhaas have argued that the discipline can best regain power by adapting itself to market tendencies and fantasies. Diller/Scofidio's recent (unbuilt) project for the CNN headquarters in Atlanta features an atrium whose translucent walls act as a gigantic television monitor: building merges with media. Koolhaas, currently designing boutiques for Prada, argues that architecture must become a high-stakes player in the game of building global image-fields, anticipating and directing flows of consumer desire. In this manner, by branding buildings with companies and their product lines, architects can help direct campaigns to capture and focus consumer attention and perception—it is going to happen with or without architects, so they might as well join the fray. This idea is, in fact, a variation of the sort of strategy that Peter Behrens used in his work for the AEG in Berlin, designing a company's logo and products as well as its buildings. But there is a contemporary twist: today the architect must attend to the popular reception of company image, products, and buildings within an intensely competitive marketplace. (Of course, architects must also resist becoming mere image-relations specialists.)

Another, more experimental idea is for architects to work within the broadest definition of "architecture." In business and especially the information economy, "architecture" designates large-scale, complex, and organized systems. This idea is not new; two centuries ago, Kant described human reason as architectonic, raising a mere aggregate of knowledge into a system. Today, "enterprise software," which coordinates all aspects of what companies do, is a new business technology intended to unify production and consumption within an efficient system. An outgrowth of enterprise software, "enterprise architecture" orchestrates the software and machine types of a particular business operation as well as the standards for designed environments (square footage, number of desks, location, etc.). What is absent from this business model is any sense or appreciation of the sensual and aesthetic, and that is a crucial omission because the design of buildings will increasingly be coordinated according to quantitative factors installed into software. Thus, the appearance of the built landscape might change dramatically if design considerations—a digitized mapping of qualitative information, so to speak—were introduced in the early stages of design rather than being left to the end in a difficult effort to aestheticize a finished product. Given the importance of image and information to marketing campaigns, this idea is not that far-fetched. Architects, after all, possess great facility in manipulating and signifying large-scale forms and spaces.

It is also time for architects to think beyond actual buildings or the exhibition of drawings and to begin creating architectural products akin to CDs or DVDs. Digital technology is on the cusp of a revolution in the construction of captivating virtual environments. Continuing the trajectory of video games, all sorts of interactive visual adventure-worlds will be manufactured in familiar and unfamiliar settings. Journeys will be made into reconstituted environs such as the fora of ancient Rome, into unbuilt projects such as Tony Garnier's Cité Industrielle, into places whose futuristic scenarios borrow from science and science fiction. Instead of traveling in the real world, we will increasingly traverse digital time and space. These cyber landscapes are like symphonies or films—constructed (and potentially interactive) narratives of space, form, color, and idea. Their implications are immense. If architects were to design cyberscapes so exciting that they commanded widespread attention, they might at the same time make buildings more relevant to the culture at large. The idea of cyberscapes does not exclude the sensate world. Rather, it presumes that screen or virtual entertainments are today's unavoidable corollary to the real built landscape. Our perception and understanding of building and landscape emerge not just from on-site engagements but more and more via the edited and de-territorialized mediations of digitized commodities.

I have argued that architects should rethink their identities and actions within the commodified built landscape. I also believe that we all should heighten our sensitivity to ordinary building. Some love its common and at times accidental beauty—the patterns of oil stains and painted lines on parking lots observed by Ed Ruscha, for instance, or the dignities of mass production and stamped machinery embraced by Ray and Charles Eames. Others despise its oppressive, materialistic banality, the congested nonplaces and overdigested marketing formulas. My own feelings waver between fascination and revulsion. The same grid of bougainvillea-draped walls, mini-malls, and aerospace sheds in a corner of Orange County, California, can appear nondescript today, captivating tomorrow. What does not change is my compulsion to look at and write about ordinary building, on both its terms and mine.

2000

Notes

1. Arjun Appadurai, *Modernity at Large: Cultural Dimensions of Globalization* (Minneapolis: University of Minnesota Press, 1996), 67.

2. Max Weber, *Economy and Society: An Outline of Interpretive Sociology*, ed. Guenther Roth and Claus Wittich, trans. Ephraim Fischoff et al. (New York: Bedminster Press, 1968), 375.

3. David Ogilvy, *Ogilvy on Advertising* (New York: Crown, 1983), 14.

4. Jean Baudrillard, *The Consumer Society: Myths and Structures* (London; Thousand Oaks, CA: Sage, 1998).

5. William Kowinski, *The Malling of America: An Inside Look at the Great Consumer Paradise* (New York: W. Morrow, 1985).

6. Malcolm Gladwell, "The Science of Shopping," *New Yorker,* November 4, 1996, www.gladwell.com/1996_1_04_a_shopping.htm.

7. Paul Virilio, *The Virilio Reader,* ed. James Der Derian (Malden, MA: Blackwell Publishers, 1998), 121.

9

Privatized Lives:
On the Embattled 'Burbs

James S. Russell

A recent *New York Times* story captures a dilemma that has become all too familiar at the developing edges of urban America. In 1978 Carol and Dennis Ferry thought they had found their close-to-nature dream when they moved from a starter home in Trenton, New Jersey, to a house on the edge of farm fields in Hamilton. But a few years later, houses covered those fields, and a drive that once took ten minutes stretched to half an hour. So the Ferrys moved to Hopewell at the rural fringe of Mercer County. But once again, their dream seems about to vanish; once again, the bulldozers can be glimpsed in the distance. The couple recently learned that they will be sharing their idyll with an office park being built by Merrill Lynch, a development that could reach 5.5 million square feet—about the size of one tower of Manhattan's World Trade Center. "Where do we go next?" Mrs. Ferry asked the reporter. "There's really no place you can go to hide."[1]

Places you can go to hide are indeed scarce in today's suburban landscape. The Ferrys have pursued the American dream, the dream of the sylvan retreat far from the restless metropolis, with unusual dedication. What is not unusual, however, is that the retreat—at least one close to urban amenities and opportunities—continues to elude them, even in a state that claims to be committed to funneling development into existing communities so that natural surroundings remain close by. As the *Times* put it: "Money and jobs—in this case the threat to move 3,500 jobs to Pennsylvania—can trump public land preservation policy."

"There's really no place you can go to hide." The Ferrys—like most Americans—are ignorant of the powerful urban development mechanisms that draw the bulldozers toward their ephemeral idyll. Their naïveté is telling. If you buy a new house in a new subdivision next to open land, what guarantees exist that the land will remain open, undeveloped, uncluttered by speculative houses and office "parks"? And yet thousands of people every year buy new houses in new communities, hoping that the view will stay the same—the oak woods will not become the Oak Woods Estates. They imagine that it is the *next* development, the place down the road, not their own, that is spoiling the pretty landscape and clogging the quiet country roads.

The Ferrys' blinkered view underscores the largely unacknowledged means by which the vast suburban landscape has been produced in the United States in the past half century and by which it is still produced. Suburbia has long outgrown commonly held frames of reference. Even the term *suburbia* no longer describes America's low-density *urb,* despite the various and regionally diverse countrified trappings. Such trappings—exemplified by the tendency to favor a small-town, country-gentry atmosphere—cause social and cultural critics to focus too closely on the presumed uniformity, conformity, and cultural narrowness of suburbia. But the communities that actually fit this mold are rare. Only the outermost belt of white-flight suburbs offers old-fashioned grist for the critical mill. We pay insufficient attention to what the new settlers of suburbia are fleeing from and why today's urban edges have mutated into such unstable and unsatisfying forms. How America builds its urban areas is *the* critical issue of the built environment at the start of the new century. Deeper pathologies are only beginning to be understood, and they will vex the nation well into the twenty-first century.

A home surrounded by lush lawns and leafy streets where children can safely play: this was the dream that inspired the great suburban building boom of the 1950s. It is a dream that retains a powerful hold on the American imagination, even as today's suburbanites admit how distant that image is from contemporary reality. Indeed, the Ferrys' choice of the word *hide* is revealing. For a long time ownership of a home on its own plot of land, a private place that could be molded to the desires of its owners, has been an emblem of freedom and individu-

"We share your dreams." Photograph by Virgil Hancock III; courtesy of Etherton Gallery.

alism. But contemporary suburbia, the land of hunkered-down gated communities and tanklike SUVs, exemplifies an era that promises less security and threatens many potential, if sometimes inchoate, dangers. Deed restrictions covering everything from paint color to roof-tile configuration to landscape features can be understood as efforts to enforce an orderliness that seems no longer to exist outside the subdivision.

Robert Fishman has written of the "powerful cultural ideal" of suburbia, its power derived "from the capacity of suburban design to express a complex and compelling vision of the modern family freed from the corruption of the city, restored to harmony with nature, endowed with wealth and independence, yet protected by a close-knit, stable community."[2] Escaping the city and finding a refuge where, as Kenneth T. Jackson put it, one could "keep the world at bay"[3] has long been a leitmotif in the cultural construction of suburbia, one that has received perilously little scrutiny. The city to which suburbia historically offered itself as the utopian opposite was noisy, congested, chaotic, amoral, unfettered, an everyone-for-himself, capitalistic free-for-all. Who could live a decent life in a restless metropolis where a smelly tannery might set up shop next to a genteel residence or where office towers clawed their way skyward without regard for how they cast their neighbors in shadows?

Corrupt the city may have been, but in its aggrandizement of individual ambition, it was purely American. But Americans also longed for orderliness and civility, which the early postwar suburbs seem to have offered. In particular, William H. Whyte's seminal sociological dissection of Park Forest, Illinois, *The Organization Man*, depicts a community of admirable solidarity.[4] Friendships were quickly formed. Doors were left unlocked. Neighbors shared babysitting duties with little fuss or formality. Early residents participated in an impressive variety of community-service activities and personal-enrichment forums. Neighbors felt comfortable entering each other's homes with only a knock and a shouted hello. So much was shared in the early years of Park Forest that residents used to joke about their "socialist" tendencies.

Of course, Park Forest was not unique. An image published in a *Time-Life* survey of the Pacific states in 1966 takes in a single block of a single subdivision called Newport Hills, in Bellevue, outside Seattle. The image and its annotations are extraordinary less for what is there than for what is not: no single people, no single parents, no elderly, no members of any nonwhite ethnic group, almost no women who worked outside the home.[5] Should the *Time-Life* editors want to recreate this scene, they would no longer be able to, even though Southeast 54th Street is as well tended today as in 1966. Indeed, they would be hard-pressed to find any place of such singular homogeneity anywhere in suburban America today.

The comforting environments of Park Forest and Newport Hills reflected less a triumph of social engineering or urban planning than a unique moment in American history. "The middle decades of the 20th century were an entirely anomalous period in American history," writes David Frum.[6] "Never had the state been so strong, never had people submitted as uncomplainingly, never had the country been more economically equal, never had it been more ethnically homogeneous, seldom was its political consensus so overpowering." Writing about another Park Forest–like Chicago suburb, author Alan Ehrenhalt describes the 1950s as an era of easy sociability and of a broadly understood ethic of civic obligation and family duty, but in *The Lost City: Discovering the Forgotten Virtues of Community in the Chicago of the 1950s*, he also finds this sort of solidarity in an urban neighborhood in southwest Chicago and even to a degree in Bronzeville—the center of Chicago's black ghetto.

In the cities, the stability and calm of the 1950s would fall victim to the enormous economic and social dislocations of later decades. The suburbs held on longer; ideals of family, closeness to nature, and commitment to community borne on the self-interest of homeownership— if on little else—were long thought to fortify the 'burbs against the social and economic vicissitudes that beset older cities. But increasingly the suburbs have been succumbing to urban maladies. As early as 1955—the last year of his research—Whyte found the impressive solidarity of Park Forest dissolving. Today, forty-four years after *The Organization Man* was published, the tidy bungalows and split-levels look surprisingly unchanged. But the local companies Whyte chronicled have closed their doors or fled, taking with them countless jobs. "For rent" banners dangle from the few office buildings nearby. The once stylish shopping center has struggled against abandonment for more than a decade. Population and household income have slid; single parents head more families than ever before. The once almost all-white suburb now boasts of its ethnic diversity, but drug addiction, racial tension, and gang activity are among the "urban" social ills that now plague this suburb.[7]

Park Forest is just one instance of the changing and diversifying fortunes of suburban communities, claims urban analyst Myron Orfield. Within the so-called favored-sector suburbs, the mid-rise offices that line the lushly landscaped arterial corridors sport the logos of high-tech and financial firms—evidence of their abundance of high-paying white-collar jobs—and nearby can be found the most expensive "executive" housing. The taxes generated by such high-value commercial and residential developments underwrite good schools, ample parks, roads, libraries, and other government services. In contrast, many older inner-ring suburbs (like Park Forest) struggle to provide good schools and government services with a tax base generated from low-priced housing, lower-tier retail, and warehouses. Emerging middle-income suburbs, at the outermost urban reaches, while not saddled with aging housing or infrastructure, rarely attract the kind of affluent residential or commercial development whose prosperity would underwrite the fast-growing demand for services and relieve the crowding at the bursting-at-the-seams schools.[8]

Orfield draws a starker picture of suburbia's future than many analysts do, but his conclusions are widely accepted in policy-making circles—if not in political ones, where the consequences are regarded as potentially explosive. Orfield sees many forces that are driving communities apart both spatially and sociologically. The favored sector encompasses the "edge cities" described by Joel Garreau.[9] This sector grew up around already wealthy areas with few tax burdens and has enjoyed the advantage of highway and airport infrastructure paid for by older communities. Favored-sector towns often defend their affluence through exclusionary zoning—keeping out apartments and small-lot developments that might draw people who consume more services than their tax payments would support. In the early postwar years, housing near jobs and good schools was readily available in the suburbs near most cities, and it was affordable on a single income. But today, in desirable metro areas like San Francisco, Los Angeles, New York, Boston, Seattle, and Portland, Oregon, median house prices are increasingly out of reach for even relatively affluent dual-income families. Other once-inexpensive communities are rapidly catching up.[10] Orfield asserts that edge cities use their wealth to offer incentives to draw businesses out of older downtowns and, nowadays, out of older suburbs (in this way edge cities maintain their tax bases without taxing their own residents and businesses too heavily). They wield their considerable political clout and thus secure the lion's share of business-attracting infrastructure.

Outside the favored sector, however, the reality is not prosperity and growth but, all too often, stagnation and decline. These more affordable communities offer less appealing subdivisions with scruffy, overcrowded schools, meager recreational amenities, significant exposure to crime, and long commutes through exasperating traffic to where the jobs are.[11] Orfield points out that while Chicago's poorest and most desolate neighborhoods occupy dozens of census tracts, struggling inner-ring suburbs comprise eighty-seven troubled communities stretching in a mind-boggling sixty-five-mile crescent from O'Hare Airport south and east into Indiana. If these and similar communities around the country continue to deteriorate, the United States could face blight and poverty on a scale that would dwarf the urban devastation of the 1960s and 1970s.

Big-city residents have long confronted dilemmas such as whether to forsake friends and urban amenities to move to a community with

"The Enclave," Princeton, New Jersey. This particular house design was deployed in 30 percent of speculative housing construction in the United States in 1999. Photograph by Phillip Jones.

good schools and safe streets. Similar dilemmas now plague suburbanites as the homogeneity and small-town ambience they sought "out there" give way to increasing sociological difference.

In 1968, in *The Private City*, historian Sam Bass Warner decried what he saw as the increasingly chaotic and fragmented urban landscape, blaming its faults on the culture of privatism, a culture that America developed very early, essentially at its founding. Although Warner was not specifically criticizing suburbia (in the book it goes largely unmentioned), his analysis of the workings of privatism and of its consequences for the urban landscape remains more compelling than ever—and relevant to the suburban landscape as well. "Psychologically, privatism meant that the individual should seek happiness in personal independence and in the search for wealth," Warner wrote. "Socially, privatism meant that the individual should see his first loyalty as his immediate family and that a community should be a union of such money-making, accumulating families; politically, privatism meant that the community should keep the peace among the individual money-makers, and, if possible, help to create an open and thriving setting where each citizen would have some substantial opportunity to prosper."[12]

The privatism that Warner analyzed notably lacks any dimension of the civic idealism that animates so many other American values. But can anyone doubt that privatism undergirds the city-making values that most Americans take for granted as fundamental, whether they actually approve of them or not? The city that Americans have so long sought to escape can in certain important ways be understood as the product of America's culture of privatization.

The promise of suburbia was that the city and its perpetual upheavals—driven by privatism—would remain a distant disturbance. But when the fast-growing and affordable bedroom communities became home to a wide swath of the middle class after the Second World War, business eventually followed the homeowners outward, inventing a new kind of low-density urbanism through a privatized ethos. Privatism in the suburbs did not evolve as it had in the cities, however, which is why it has been so difficult to recognize its capacity to destroy precisely what people came to suburbia in search of.

In suburbia, belching factories did not rise up cheek by jowl with fetid tenements. As commercial and institutional uses located outside cities, suburbia spawned its most emblematic form: the opportunistic strip, in which the buildings were oriented only to the convenience of the automobile. The fundamental element of modern low-density urbanism is not the single-family house on the quarter-acre plot, not the cul-de-sac lined with single-family houses, but rather the multilane 40- to 60-mph arterial road. In privatized suburbia's simplest manifestations, a developer erects a building in the middle of a plot along this well-traveled street and blacktops the surrounding acreage. Each element of urban development—residential subdivision, fast-food outlet, ball field, or office park—is ranged podlike along the arterial. Auto access is carefully considered; the prospect of arrival by bus, by bicycle, or on foot is almost always ignored. Such developments were inevitably conceived individualistically, in no way acknowledging their neighbors on the adjacent plot. Strip developers made no attempt to create a coherent urbanistic assemblage. Andres Duany and other New Urbanists demonstrate the folly of such "planning" by showing the convoluted route a condominium dweller must take (inevitably by car) out of the condo development onto the arterial and into the feeder and parking system of an adjacent mall. The actual destination may be 150 feet away as the crow flies, but easy access is blocked by the lack of connection between the development and the other suburban pods.[13]

And, of course, not only are civic places, workplaces, recreational places, and places of residence rarely integrated within suburbia, they are also often separated by great distances. What unites suburbia is not shared public space or a coherent architectural vision but a vast, civil-engineered network of roads. In fact, to the extent that architecture or design is deployed in suburbia at all, it is deployed as advertising—as packaging to attract the passing motorist; to the extent that any suburb possesses a sense of place, it does so because of the preserved (for the moment) features of its native landscape or because of a parklike treatment of roads.

Before the era of the automobile, the necessity of density and proximity produced cities with a consistent and efficient street-oriented fabric that offered a rich variety of experiences. Public spaces were seen as the inevitable and desirable extensions of private spaces, which were often small and crowded. You used the porch, the stoop, or the street to socialize, to play, to beat the summer heat, or to simply to escape the suffocating embrace of family. Citizens learned to observe a range of social norms of language, manner, and dress that ordered the shared public realm. And one of those norms required that the buildings themselves be dressed in an architecture that at least would make a minimal gesture to decorum and that at best—in the great railway stations, the urban park systems, the museums, monuments, and civic gateways—might brilliantly represent community aspiration or create a place with a distinct and memorable identity.

By contrast, the privatized model of urban development embodies no nonmercantile aspirations. Suburbia today conforms to a simplistic, low-density, auto-dependent, money-driven model. True, certain aspirations are satisfied in the provision of residential and commercial structures that reflect consumer taste. Nonetheless, what one drives by in the typical American suburb is the result of little more than thousands of purely economic transactions. And in this instrumental landscape, each individual development is manufactured and considered only within its own short-term economic parameters. Any sense of a larger community or shared culture must struggle against the physical impediments of distance and the devotion to the automobile. Architect and planner William Morrish helps neighborhoods understand these consequences by creating maps showing libraries and parks. These often appear in easy proximity to residents, until—in the "aha!"

moment—he overlays the arterials and freeways that separate houses from these important public places and thus form the psychological if not physical barriers within their communities.[14]

In the past quarter century, places like Atlanta, Houston, Dallas, Phoenix, and Los Angeles have become incomprehensibly vast suburban metropolises, offering a full range of urban employment, housing, and recreational opportunities. Silicon Valley in California, Westchester County in New York, the northern Virginia suburbs of Washington, and the beltway suburbs of Boston have become wealth-creating powerhouses, with economies comparable to those of entire nations. American suburbia has assumed the mercantile functions of the once-distant city and has reaped the benefits, offering diverse economic opportunity and generous government services. But the benefits have come at a high cost: in recent years perils once confined largely to the city—poverty, crime, traffic congestion, pollution, failing schools, frightening otherness, anonymity—have invaded the once tranquil leafy streets.

The cacophonous, fragmented landscape of today's low-density urbanism would be unrecognizable to such spiritual godfathers of suburbia as Andrew Jackson Davis, Frederick Law Olmsted, and Calvert Vaux. Today few suburbs remain only bedroom communities, reliant on a nearby metropolis for shopping and working. Indeed, as Fishman argued in *Bourgeois Utopias,* the postwar suburban era ended as bedroom communities became urban places in their own right. What is emerging in its place continues to confound us. Although New Urbanism has addressed the public/private equation at the neighborhood level, its long-term viability as a development model remains unproved. No method or mentality—no planning technique, no social consensus, no cultural tradition—has yet been devised to create a workably expressive *suburban* urbanism at a scale larger than that of the individual subdivision or office park, an urbanism that would reproduce the rich array of street rituals that were created for the city.

Fishman, like many students of suburbia, cites Frank Lloyd Wright's Broadacre City as a model for an integrated vision of the low-density city where people live, work, and enjoy a civic identity. With its picturesque groupings of buildings separated by swaths of greenery, Broadacre City offered a powerful visual ideal; in privatized America, however, it is an ideal that cannot be realized.

Hoffman Estates, Illinois, 1993. Photograph copyright by Bob Thall.

Within the apparent tranquility of their tract-house realms, sub-urbanites rarely recognize that the individualistic, privatized ethos so powerfully embodied by the house on the lawn is exactly the ethos that regularly upends the sense of carefully constructed gentility and orderliness that constitutes one of the chief attractions of suburbia. The culture of privatism allows citizens to consider their house as their castle, but the gates and deeded covenants cannot prevent Merrill Lynch from moving in next door. Writ large, the rights of owners to do whatever they want to do with their property has produced the freewheeling growth machine that now produces the same relentless and upsetting change that people left the city to escape.[15]

Private-sector real-estate investment and development are forces propelling worldwide urban growth, but the relationship between the private and the public sectors in the United States is unique and has never been much accepted in the rest of the world. To varying degrees other countries envision city form and growth as representative of community values rather than of an accumulation of individual de-cisions. So government is empowered far more directly to plan and guide growth. Some countries and cities have a long history of centralized control of development; some cultures, such as the Japanese, rank the values of the community much higher than the interests of the individual or the family; some cultures regard the extended family as more important than the nuclear family. Indeed, the American emphasis on independent individual action is viewed as downright dangerous in many religious cultures.

Even in democratic and capitalist countries—the Netherlands, Germany, and Scandinavia come to mind—government often determines which cities will grow, where they will grow, and by how much and with what design. Dutch people need not move every few years in search of a less-degraded landscape, because private development is channeled by the public sector to maintain an ordered community. America has never entrusted such powers to public agencies. Although local and state governments in the United States employ city planners, their powers, never impressive, have been eviscerated over the past decade or so as the public distrust of government intervention has waxed. Even in places like Portland, Oregon, where a consensus supports such innovations as urban growth boundaries and transit-oriented development, planning remains largely a reactive enterprise. Thus, privatism remains the underlying driver of American city making, even as urban growth brings together more and more people who share fewer and fewer values, thus creating sharper conflicts. In the meantime, the enormous scale of corporations and the world economy has enabled landowners and developers to bring immense resources to the task of altering the landscape to privatized ends.

The failure to reconcile the role of a privatized economy with the desire for an ordered, pleasant, and harmonious urbanism continues to diminish the quality of life in the United States. The "creative destruction" of capitalism has everywhere left its mark on the landscape, whether in the obvious form of abandoned malls, in the dispiriting and enervating disjunctions of opportunistic development, or in the more subtle failure of many communities to build parks, schools, and libraries. Too often these marks are permanent. And so suburbanites, increasingly overwhelmed by the disturbing forces of large-scale development, have begun to react the way city dwellers once did. Some, like the Ferrys, keep moving farther out, contributing to an immense, stunningly inefficient, and apparently perpetual population shift.

Others choose to stay and fight. Some communities have adopted antigrowth initiatives, imposed moratoriums, planted a thicket of regulations, and tacked on impact fees (requiring developers to pay for the infrastructure associated with their projects) and exactions (requiring developers to pay for this new school or that new park).

William Fulton, a chronicler of Southern California's perpetual land-use battles, sees the real estate industry as a victim of the very American dream that has made it rich. Developers are eager to point out the hypocrisy of the residents of Pine Knoll Estates who organize to stop the development of nearby Pleasant Meadow Manors. Yet, as Fulton notes, it was developers who promoted the "anti-urban bias, the small-town atmosphere, localized governments" of the privatized suburban realm.[16] Given that the Irvine Company, which built much of Orange County, California, lured buyers with the slogan "Come to Irvine to hear the asparagus grow," should it have been surprised when residents tried to stop the company from plowing under the asparagus fields?[17]

Indeed, according to Fulton, the antisprawl movement is simply the most obvious sign that the consensus that made suburbia easy and affordable to develop is evaporating. "Current property owners and residents," Fulton explains, "paid higher taxes to support the debt-financed construction of new facilities (roads, water pipes, parks, etc.) to be used by newcomers who would then help finance the next phase, and so on." (Fulton calls this an urban-development Ponzi scheme—a unwitting civic version of the classic bunko racket invented in the 1920s by Charles Ponzi, who fraudulently paid old "investors" with money from new "investors.") In the late 1970s, the passage of California's Proposition 13—the vanguard of the tax revolts of the 1980s—took the first shot at the old suburban-development consensus. Proposition 13 exempted existing residents from dramatic tax increases, but in doing so it deprived developers of the infrastructure-extension cash on which speculative construction depends. Lacking alternatives, says Fulton, local governments have pushed these costs onto developers, who must pay for all the community infrastructure related to their developments, which can be $30,000 to $40,000 per housing unit.[18]

Developers have lamented that these kinds of tax initiatives push housing costs beyond the reach of average people—"average people," in this case, being almost everyone who does not already own a neatly mowed piece of the American dream—but long-term residents, whose tax bills had been spiraling ever upward to pay for new people to move in and "ruin the place," would retort that it was only fair that the costs be borne by those who would encroach upon their idyll. Similar battles have been fought in community after community across the country. Whichever side wins a given battle, the costs are high. And no one is really winning in the end: too often the outcome is greater spatial and income division and ever more sprawl, as developers look ever farther away for land developable at lower costs and with fewer regulations.

Growing social polarization has set suburb against suburb, and the ethos of privatism not only exacerbates the conflicts but also impedes their resolution. Mamaroneck, New York, recently proposed a law—over the objections of adjacent Mount Vernon, Yonkers, White Plains, New Rochelle, and Port Chester—that would require developers to obtain Mamaroneck's approval for projects just outside its borders. Attempting to preserve its slow-paced, small-town feel, Mamaroneck wants to stop construction of an Ikea superstore in New Rochelle because the store would generate additional traffic within Mamaroneck. Poorer New Rochelle needs the tax proceeds. Not far away, Mount Vernon is in a border war with adjacent Pelham, which wants a Target store. Nearby Yonkers, a struggling industrial river town, has had to defend a superstore development in a dispute with the neighboring towns of Greenburgh, Hastings-on-Hudson, and Ardsley.[19]

Why can't these communities work together to resolve their differences? Or, more rationally, why isn't Westchester County (which encompasses all these towns) planning to equitably distribute the burdens and benefits of growth? Because the affluence and indeed the very existence of privileged communities depend on their home-rule autonomy (and, not incidentally, upon their rich tax base). So Mamaroneck pursues its legally questionable strategy, and the disputes go on and on—just as they do all across the United States.

In other ways, too, the cultures of individualism and privatism undermine the very values that animate the suburban dream. "Big-box" stores—the gigantic warehouses surrounded by asphalt acreage like Wal-Mart or Price Club—have become the vanguard of urban sprawl, shiny brand-name blemishes on suburbia's civic aspirations. However, such projects generate so much sales tax revenue that communities compete desperately to lure them. Fulton documents how the post–Proposition 13 political landscape in California (in which sales taxes have become the most important kind of local tax) has all but forced three communities into a cutthroat battle for large-scale retail *that its growth-averse citizens did not even want.*[20]

Although the neighboring cities of Oxnard, Ventura, and Camarillo had planning policies supporting reinvestment in their older downtowns, Ventura, in the 1980s, encouraged big-box retailers to line its freeway frontage in order to harvest desperately needed sales taxes from passing drivers. Oxnard followed, first subsidizing the development of an auto mall, then underwriting the construction of a "super regional" mall (which predictably but ironically threatened two existing malls, one of which was in Oxnard). The proposal collapsed, a victim of the real estate recession of the early 1990s (though the city was left holding the bag on a multimillion-dollar infrastructure investment and bonds), but it was succeeded by a "power center" proposal comprising a collection of large-scale discounters (again partially underwritten by the city) and a factory-outlet strip. Then Camarillo joined the fray, subsidizing an outlet center of its own.

By the early 1990s, Ventura's 1970s Buenaventura Mall was reeling under pressure from its new competition. Trying to save the mall, the city offered to turn over to redevelopers up to $30 million in tax revenues that would be generated by doubling the size of Buenaventura. Oxnard countered with a proposal to build a new "town center" mall. Both proposals ultimately withered, but each entailed costly lawsuits, contentious hearings, and local votes. Three cities that had hoped to maintain a less urban, quasi-agricultural landscape at the edge of the Los Angeles megalopolis ended up with ten miles of traffic-generating, could-be-anywhere sprawl along their freeways. Governments gambled taxpayers' dollars playing retail poker—a game they were ill-equipped to play, one forced upon them by the fragmented "small town" governance of America.

In the Darwinian environment of modern suburbia, the most affluent communities would seem to come out the winners. But even amid the once pastoral landscapes of privilege, life is hardly sweet these days. A high percentage of the nation's growth is occurring in these precincts, and so the green spaces that for decades defined their laid-back, bridle-pathed atmosphere are disappearing, replaced by ever larger-scaled construction (for instance, McMansions) and road-rage-inducing traffic. (And since the privileged sector has more jobs than residents, its "migrant" workers—for instance, commuters crossing the thirty miles of the Twin Cities metro area to Minneapolis's western suburbs, or slogging the seventy-five freeway miles from Moreno Valley, in Riverside County, to Universal City, in Los Angeles—clog the local expressways and parkways.) While America at large has experienced impressive economic growth in the past few years, the growth rate in the privileged sector has been torrid. Across the nation, urban development has gobbled land at a much faster rate than population growth alone would predict, and Americans are driving many more miles than they used to. In response to the development pressures generated by such phenomena, affluent Americans—who have benefited most from urban sprawl—have been in the vanguard of the antisprawl movement.

Modern suburbia is rich in such ironies. The business community that is often fingered as the instigator of sprawl has begun to recognize that unfettered, simplistic urban development may kill the economic goose that has laid America's golden eggs. Consider Silicon Valley, the forty-mile corridor of office parks and executive housing south of San Francisco. Computer and software businesses have created an economic juggernaut of unprecedented size in this emblematic low-density landscape, an economy based on an ethos of easy auto access and cheap, garaged-based creativity. Today, this vast conurbation reels in the face of sclerotic freeways, declining air quality and open space, and median house prices pushing half a million dollars. While highly paid software engineers can afford the stratospheric prices of nearby homes, all kinds of support jobs go begging because people cannot get to them from affordable communities. (Only in Silicon Valley could the *New York Times* find people earning $50,000 per year who cannot afford housing.)[21] Today business and civic groups support the antisprawl agenda of affordable housing and greater transit access—exactly the kinds of incursions such communities have long fought. It is, in fact, unclear whether business groups can get residential communities to accept change that has historically been regarded as threatening to their property values and generous public services.

For suburbia to evolve to a more stable and satisfying urban form, the United States must be prepared to consider the true field of suburban concern as larger than the subdivision or village. It must also recognize that suburban towns and cities are parts of larger regional conurbations that must be participated in, planned for, and governed as such. Americans would do well to put aside their knee-jerk anti-urbanism and consider what kind of urban place they would really like to inhabit, and, like city dwellers through the ages, consider what they are willing to give up for what they will get. Suburbanites have resisted higher-density, multifamily housing and mixed incomes and mixed uses because these are emblems of the chaotic and disordered city. But the disorder of urban life has long been threatening suburbia precisely because Americans have been unwilling to reconsider the lack of order implicit in the purely mercantile model of city making. The unit of simplistic real estate development is the increment by which the suburbs grow, but it is also what prevents the attainment of traditional urbanity or civility. America need not attempt to re-create a nostalgic urban vision or to follow modern European models. The nation may well develop a new path, even a unique path, if we are willing to try.

Urban planning as currently conceived is not up to the task. Planning in modern urban America is almost entirely reactive, almost entirely devoted to promulgating regulations intended to prevent the last problem from repeating itself. Thus has the nation created a regulatory apparatus as complex and unwieldy as it is ineffective. Policy makers have proposed tax-base sharing among adjacent suburbs and metro-area governance as a means to coordinate development among communities, but the ideal of small-town home rule is so deeply embedded in the suburban psyche that any such solutions face extraordinary hurdles. Even Portland, Oregon, lauded as a model of sensible planning, has had to fight three initiatives that sought to dismantle its regional-planning process.

There are those who welcome America's privatized urban-growth model because they believe it encourages creativity and innovation. Certainly it has incidentally provided such durable urban forms as the loft building and the townhouse row. But many Americans seek more order and predictability in their environs than most cities typically provide, and it is this group that is fleeing older communities and colonizing new ones on the developing edge. Their desires must somehow be accommodated.

Growth pressure is not letting up, and, like a river, it flows over and around obstacles, seeking the path of least resistance. Rather than battle antigrowth activists or jump through constricting regulatory hoops, developers simply move outward until they find a place more congenial to unimpeded growth. In Southern California, says Fulton, that means "halfway to Las Vegas," if not Las Vegas itself. Indeed, Fulton sees the desert metropolis, 250 miles east of the Hollywood Bowl, as a satellite of Los Angeles, flung a once unimaginable distance from its parent. In Las Vegas, acres of tile-roofed new housing march into the red rock desert, filling with legions of immigrants who seek the dream Los Angeles no longer promises. How long until their numbers swell to the point that, like the Ferrys, they seek yet another place of refuge?

2000

Notes

1. Iver Peterson, "In New Jersey, Sprawl Keeps Outflanking Its Foes," *New York Times,* March 17, 2000, A1.

2. Robert Fishman, *Bourgeois Utopias: The Rise and Fall of Suburbia* (New York: Basic Books, 1987), x.

3. Kenneth T. Jackson, *The Crabgrass Frontier: The Suburbanization of the United States* (New York: Oxford, 1985), 48.

4. William H. Whyte, *The Organization Man* (New York: Simon & Schuster, 1956).

5. *American Library: The Pacific States* (New York: Time-Life Books, 1966), 130–31.

6. David Frum, *How We Got Here: The Seventies, the Decade That Brought You Modern Life* (New York: Basic Books, 1999), quoted in the *New Yorker*, June 5, 2000, 87.

7. Urban analyst Myron Orfield (citation below) first drew the author's attention to Park Forest's current ills. Additional information was obtained during a visit in 1999 and an interview with Village Manager Janet Muchnik.

8. Myron Orfield, *Metropolitics: A Regional Agenda for Community and Stability* (Washington, DC: Brookings Institution Press, 1997).

9. Joel Garreau, *Edge Cities: Life on the New Frontier* (New York: Doubleday, 1991).

10. The National Association of Home Builders tracks this trend through its Housing Opportunity Index.

11. Census trends show Americans moving to the largest metro areas, which offer the most job opportunities but also have the most expensive housing. Metro areas with high median income often include communities that are "affordable" but poor and crime ridden, including deteriorated central-city neighborhoods, older industrial satellite towns, and failing older suburbs (per Orfield, *Metropolitics*).

12. Sam Bass Warner, *The Private City: Philadelphia in Three Periods of Its Growth* (Philadelphia: University of Pennsylvania Press, 1968), 3. Philadelphia, the better neighborhoods of which today are regarded as models of urban design excellence, was castigated for the bleak urban landscape its privatized growth patterns created. Nevertheless, the factors Warner documented certainly contributed to the city's precipitous decline during the 1970s and 1980s, which was not of course obvious to Warner at the time.

13. See Andres Duany, Elizabeth Plater-Zyberk, and Jeff Speck, *Suburban Nation: The Rise of Sprawl and the Decline of the American Dream* (New York: North Point Press, 2000), 25.

14. Demonstrated in a talk given at the Congress of the New Urbanism, June 2000.

15. See John R. Logan and Harvey L. Molotch, *Urban Fortunes: The Political Economy of Place* (Berkeley: University of California Press, 1987), chapter 3.

16. William Fulton, *The Reluctant Metropolis* (Point Arena, CA: Solano Press, 1997), 17.

17. Ibid., 15.

18. William Fulton, interview by author.

19. Lisa W. Foderaro, "Affluent Town Seeks to Curb Development Outside Its Borders," *New York Times*, March 11, 2000, B1.

20. Fulton, *The Reluctant Metropolis*, chapter 10.

21. Evelyn Nieves, "Many in Silicon Valley Cannot Afford Housing, Even at 50,000 a Year," *New York Times*, February 20, 2000, A20.

10

Duct Tape Nation:
Land Use, the Fear Factor,
and the New Unilateralism
Andrew Ross

In the fall of 2002, a pair of snipers brought terror to the suburban strongholds around Washington, DC, claiming as many as ten victims over several weeks. A striking consequence of their shooting spree was the spectacle of suburbanites driving to urban gas pumps to fill up their tanks, ostensibly because they believed the city was the only safe place to get out of their cars in public. It was an image that spoke volumes about the geography of safety in the United States now, especially if you consider how heavily racialized that geography is. Not long after the

A gated community in Dana Point, California, ca. 1980s or 1990s. Photograph by Macduff Evertone/CORBIS.

110

snipers were apprehended, Patricia Williams wrote an incisive column in *The Nation* comparing the media speculation about them when they were still at large—that the shootings were the work of a white Lone Ranger, probably an ex-Marine, and therefore a canny maestro of guerilla tactics and weaponry—and the resulting media coverage when it transpired that they were black—which suggested that they had been incompetent, committing blunder after blunder in their trail of mayhem.

Suburban profiling is not exactly geared toward African Americans. In that neck of the woods, when bullets start flying, the finger on the trigger is usually white-skinned. Downsized middle managers, with nothing to show for twenty years of deferential service, or repressed school kids, allegedly under the influence of figures like Marilyn Manson, are more and more likely to be the suspects of choice. Accordingly, the psychological roots of the snipers' motivation have not generated any of the national soul searching and hand-wringing that followed the Columbine High School massacre. In the imagination of white America, it is more or less taken for granted that black folks dream of taking potshots at white targets and that these fantasies would come to be realized on occasion. Even so, the prospect of a guerrilla race war in the suburbs is too far-fetched, or else too terrifying, to contemplate, so the racial dimension of the shootings was easily dismissed as an aberration.

The spectacle of anxious SUV owners at the gas pumps is another story, however. For one thing, it is a much more articulate image than that of the World Trade Center crumbling. It speaks directly to the high cost of maintaining the culture of suburban land development, driven, in part, by fear (of the city) and built around an infrastructure that is utterly dependent on the free flow of cheap oil. By force of habit, we think of the urban skyscraper as the most characteristic American legacy—or trademark. In retrospect, the Twin Towers have often been cited as the quintessential American target. Yet arguably the more distinctive emblem of American civilization has been its postwar suburban landscape—the formulaic subdivisions, with their cookie-cutter quarter-acre lots, arterial road systems, and ever-mutating strip malls. After all, the United States was an urban nation only between the 1920 and the 1970 censuses. However energy efficient it was during those years, as a majority suburban nation for the past three decades it has far outrun all other countries in unsustainability.

Usually it is up to urbanists to make the connections between the skyscrapers and the subdivisions, but the petroleum-happy Bush administration has been doing that job with aplomb ever since 9/11. Though the Twin Towers would hardly have benefited from such protection, the new Department of Homeland Security took the step of advising homeowners to wrap their houses in plastic sheeting and duct tape. This ludicrous tip resulted in a hysteric run on Home Depots (or Home Despots as they are known in my household) that are the retail bastion of every respectable suburban mall. One bittersweet Internet parody had Christo wrap the White House. But the current prime occupant of that building is the mouthpiece of what many see as a much larger program for consumerism. The intentionally vague profile of Bush's infinite war against terrorism now guarantees a truly permanent war economy in a way that the cold war version could not.

Why is this so important? It is a given wisdom that U.S. consumers are the patrons of last resort for the world economy. But no consumer in the world is more reliable than the U.S. military, whose budget has been a paragon of stability for fifty years in an economic system prone to overproduction and underconsumption. When Eisenhower issued his famous warning about the power of the military-industrial complex, he was cautioning against the overt influence of the military lobby in politics, not about its crucial role as an economic stabilizer. Without the Pentagon's budget, after all, none of the R & D for the information revolution would have been undertaken at the expense of American taxpayers. In retrospect, the New Economy of the 1990s—when technological innovation was financed by private venture capital—may have been a brief interregnum between two long phases of military Keynesianism.

Few people remember—unlike Eisenhower's caveat—Harry Truman's more persistent warnings about the influence of the real estate lobby, a formidable coalition consisting of the trade associations of petroleum producers, auto manufacturers, road builders, home builders, land developers, real estate brokers, tire makers, and several other industrial players. The coordinated power of this lobby ensured that the development of cheap farmland into a conventional suburban landscape would prove a dependable engine of consumption, year in and year out. Nor was this process any less subsidized by the state, which backed every aspect of the package in a politicized bid to boost private home ownership almost exclusively, in its definitive phase, for white families. (William Levitt, the grandee of cold war suburbanization, famously said, "A man with a plot of ground of his own is not fodder for the Communist Party or the American Labor Party.") To this day, the tax exemption for single-family-home mortgage holders is the third biggest federal money sink, next to the military appropriation and payments for Medicaid and Medicare.

While another petroleum war continues in the Middle East, it would be callous to ignore the implications of those policies that linked cold war militarization and suburbanization. They were the twin economic anchors of the Pax Americana, and, to the degree that they still are, they are a clear and present danger to anyone unlucky enough to get in the way of the fuel that supplies their energy needs. From the perspective of Kyoto-abiding citizens elsewhere, resistance to Dubya's invasion of Iraq has boiled down to a very simple question: why should the rest of the world be held hostage by the energy budget of the three-car American suburban home? It is a question that cuts through much of the thick fog generated by the miasmal debates about the new geopolitics of unilateralism preached by hawks in the Bush Administration.

That said, no serious scholar should let pass the crude generalizations that are ritually made about the shape and content of suburbia. The landscape, the population, and the folkways are much too various these days to admit loose talk about a singular "suburban way of life." Even so, urban studies are still permeated by an antisuburban prejudice, sorely reflected in the lack of literature that looks the subdivision squarely in the eye. Ethnographic studies of suburban life are scarce compared to the voluminous accounts of inner-city communities and urban subcultures. An egregious case in point is the population of gated communities, which has registered the most rapid recent growth among U.S. settlements—from four million in 1995 to roughly seventeen million (over 6 percent of the U.S. population) in 2001. In some regions, one in ten people lives behind gates. This phenomenon has elicited exactly one scholarly book to date, *Fortress America*, Edward Blakely and Mary Gail Snyder's fast-moving typology of the variety of gated forms.[1] Now, with the recent publication of Setha Low's *Behind the Gates*, we have an ethnography that focuses on the psychology of the residents themselves.[2] Does her method offer a better understanding of the appeal of these fortified havens and the external factors driving their mercurial growth?

In following the vogue for multisited ethnography, Low forsakes the detailed "thick" description of a single setting for a range of different locations: some on New York's Long Island, several others near San Antonio, Texas, and one in Mexico City. This choice turns out to be fruitful. Whatever profundity she loses from a close residential study of a bounded community is outweighed by the insights about regional differences that her research uncovers.

In the politically liberal Northeast, for example, where taxation is widely accepted as a fact of citizenship, she finds that the primary motivations of gated residents are attaining social status and reducing conflict in their lives to a manageable minimum. With their own management contractors and home-owner association rules, these communities are prized as smoothly running vehicles of impersonal governance. In the conservative Sunbelt regions, where income tax is regarded as the spawn of Satan, gated communities are favored as the most efficient and cost-effective way of providing services. Regions drawing on a tax base limited by a right-wing political climate cannot readily cope with rapid growth, and so they look to land-use mechanisms like the gated community to take on the job. In the Mexico City location, where the state cannot guarantee public policing let alone reliable services, the gates are the only way, for residents who can afford them, of securing both. Even at that, the closed condominium is vulnerable to the temptations of its own workers, as one resident reported: "People would go to church, and when they came back they would find their house empty" (128).

While this regional variation is illuminating, Low finds more predictable features widely shared. Some of these, as it happens, rest on an entirely mythical foundation. For example, Low reports that no statistical evidence exists for the universal belief that homes behind gates retain their value better over time (24). Nor does she find any evidence to support the notion that gates deter crime. Crime rates behind gates do not differ significantly from those in ungated neighboring communities. On occasion, the high visibility of the security measures actually engenders crime. As Low muses, the gates "may contribute to placing residents at increased risk by marking the community as a wealthy enclave where burglary is lucrative" (224). But for the most part, where crime rates are lower, it is because gated communities tend to be located in areas where crime is already rare. In other words, there is no immediate environmental rationale for the siege mentality that thrives behind the gates. Even in the cities, crime rates have been dropping for a decade in inverse proportion to the tabloid media's deepening addiction to fear-mongering headlines ("if it bleeds, it leads"). So what lies behind the phobic tales collected in this book? Why on earth, when the actual statistics about child abduction by nonfamily members are so low, are middle-class parents so concerned about their tykes being snatched that they would discourage them from leaving the house at all, even in a gated community with professional security patrols?

The easiest answer to this conundrum is that perception is everything. The raw psychosocial material that feeds off imagined threats is all too easily manipulated into phobic forms. In the kind of "risk society" that Ulrich Beck has written so well about, social status is earned and maintained by establishing immunity to risk.[3] Privilege is defined not by your assumed wealth and power but by your perceived level of invulnerability to risk, and every little detail adds up. National security is this immunity writ large, and especially when the state policy of the world's only superpower increasingly expresses the same aspiration on behalf of all its citizens. With the advent of the so-called war on terror, the U.S. government's legitimacy no longer derives from its capacity or willingness to ensure a decent standard of living for those citizens; it depends, instead, on the degree to which they can be successfully persuaded they are on the verge of being terrorized. In this scenario, threats are much more valuable than assets. After all, a nation bent on monopolizing power for itself needs foes (concocted ones if necessary) much more than it needs allies, and in the shadowy figure of the modern terrorist, hawks have found a perfectly pliable one.

Just as the proliferation of weaponry generates new anxieties about vulnerability (do we really have enough to fight two major wars at the same time?), the gates around a community can act as a worry catalyst rather than as a pacifier. In Low's survey, some residents confess that what they worry most about is the false sense of security provided by the gates; that is, it is actually more vexing to live with the illusion that you are safe than to live in a truly unsafe environment. In fact, when all is said and done, it might be more psychologically reassuring to do it on the cheap; faux gates (without guards) are sprouting up all over suburbia, creating the mere appearance of security, or status, for the gateless. Or it may be more effective to go anti-gate, as New Urbanists have done. In the course of the year I spent in Disney's town of Celebration, collecting material for my book *The Celebration Chronicles*, I heard a panoply of stories about the relationship between design and security. As an ostensibly New Urbanist town, Celebration has a physical plan and a citizenly ethos committed to a public culture that is the antithesis of the gated community. Yet most people who had heard of the town automatically assumed it was gated, and many of those who visited concluded that the security, even if it was invisible, was still massive. In fact, the police presence was light, and there were no downtown cameras; it was community self-surveillance that was all-powerful. Despite the town's come-hither to utter strangers, the crime rate (with the possible exception of "domestic abuse") was not notable. Many residents had moved there from gated communities, and they fervently wanted to prove that their families would develop a healthier social attitude toward others in a pedestrian-friendly environment where folks looked out for each other. Their evangelical belief helped to make it so, perhaps more than did the physical design of the town.

Low is careful to note that when her informants talk about security, it often means different things: privacy, physical safety, community, emotional shelter. She devotes a good deal of attention to the latter, especially to the thesis, which she seems to favor above all, that residents are trying to re-create the protective havens of their childhoods. Yet this comes off as her least persuasive line of inquiry, in part because it is mixed up with a subnarrative, running through the book, about her relationship with her own sister, who is a resident in one of the Texas gated communities. This narrative thread is driven by a fairly predictable question: how could the sisters have ended up wanting such different things from life? The tug of wills between the two runs throughout the book and ends on the last page with exactly the confession that Low seems to want to hear from her sibling: "The irony is that we are trapped behind our own gates, unable to exit. Instead of keeping people out, we have shut ourselves in" (232). Rhetorically cute as a last judgment, the comment does not, however, do justice to the rich psychology of the gate suggested at other points in the volume.

More convincing are the book's ruminations about the privatization of services that ensure the basic security of citizens. The recent escalation in the promotion of fear by the media and the government may bear little relation to reality, but it has helped neoliberals shift the costs of securing services out of the purview of public provision and into the private sector. (The exceptions are those sectors of government activity subject to militarization, viz. the new empire of appropriations carved out for Homeland Security.) To hasten this transfer of responsibility, the state has needed to present itself as overburdened and inadequate in the face of spiraling obligations and expenses.

Every step of the way toward the fully marketized Nirvana has been paved by warnings about an alleged surplus of demands made upon the state, and each reduction of services has been accompanied by homilies about the superior virtues of individual responsibility. The result has been rapid class polarization, and its geographical mark is enclosure. Historically speaking, the United States has not been a land of fences. Under the pressure of privatization, the walled compounds once the sole preserve of the wealthy are now working their way into the lives of the middle classes. In each part of the country, the rationale for the enclosures has taken different forms, depending on the local political climate. Though Low does not develop this argument, the regional variation—from Mexico to New York—that she detects may turn out to be a rough geographical sketch of the uneven development of neoliberal privatization, whose most dramatic penetration so far has been in Central and Latin America (see Teresa Caldeira's revealing study of São Paolo in *City of Walls*).[4]

If that is the case, then perhaps we need to further modify our earlier parochial assumption about the presumed culpability of the American suburban home for the current state of global instability. Condemning U.S. consumers for their profligate lifestyle is a rather ancient sport, and a tolerably honorable one at that. But it is also a lazy game and, like some strains of anti-Americanism, a distraction from understanding the structural sources of the unsustainability of a market civilization. Just as the gated community has helped *create* insecurity in the minds of its residents, so too we need to see how the steady, if patchy, march of neoliberal policies is creating insecurity throughout the world, by enclosing the commons, shifting public goods and resources into private treasuries, and sacralizing property value at the expense of all other citizen rights. These policies are no more a response to real threats than the gates are, but the manipulation of fear and instability has made them into brutally efficient vehicles for the redistribution of wealth.

A less obvious way of exploring these conjectures about security would be to look at another mercurial growth pattern in U.S. exurban settlement—the rise of the mobile home. Despite the fact that by 2000, mobile homes accounted for 30 percent of all new single-family houses sold nationwide, the trend has elicited hardly any serious study.[5] On the face of it, the obverse of the gated community should be the trailer park, as it is still commonly known, despite strenuous efforts to change the nomenclature (*manufactured housing* is the preferred phrase of the mobile home industry). Stereotypes about mobile homes die hard: they are still widely regarded as wobbly boxes incapable of retaining property value, home to transient ne'er-do-wells ("trailer trash") with their resident pathologies ("hotbeds of sex and violence"), and—as firetraps and tornado magnets—unsafe at any price. Built, sold, taxed, and financed like cars and parked on leased land, they have the status of personal (not real) property and so have neither the legal surety nor the solid manifestation of security evinced by the more palatial residences in Low's book. So what does the booming popularity of this housing stock have to say about the neoliberal obsession with security? Does it undermine our assumptions about the reasons for the rise of gated communities, or is it just another story about the increasing unaffordability of the fully equipped American Dream?

John Fraser Hart, Michelle Rhodes, and John Morgan, authors of the recent study *The Unknown World of the Mobile Home,* are not particularly interested in questions like these. This is unfortunate, given the scarcity of literature on the mobile home phenomenon. Their workmanlike survey of its history and currency is primarily aimed at hosing away the barnacle-like stereotypes. The story they tell is of the mobile home's rise to respectability: from its origins in the recreational trailer of the 1920s ("a wooden tent on wheels") to its Depression status as a last resort for shelter, its wartime function as reliable source of semipermanent residence, and its gradual postwar ascendancy from dependable, affordable housing to the upscale, fully customized mini-mansion. With a peculiar but unmistakable air of pride, Hart, Rhodes, and Morgan report that today's mobile home category stretches to cover $300,000 multisectionals with indoor swimming pools and that some mobile parks are themselves gated communities with all of the luxury amenities enjoyed by high-end property owners. In this same boosterish vein, they allege, insistently, that pride of ownership runs high among many mobile dwellers, that mobility is a misnomer (since most homeowners never shift locations), and that the sense of community is often much stronger than in the more elite residential enclaves that the industry now seeks to emulate. When you put the case so cheerfully, who would plump for the high sticker price and the property taxes of a site-built home? Mobile home builders could hardly have hoped for better PR from a scholarly book.

As the industry tries to move upmarket, its hunger for larger profit margins is putting the squeeze on the already shrinking availability of

Upscale trailer park, Newberg, Oregon. Photograph by Bruce Forster/STONE.

affordable housing. Even so, the bulk of mobile stock still lies in the lower income range, and its popularity cannot be disconnected from the decreasing financial fortune of the lower middle class over the past two decades. In many parts of the country (and again, the regional irregularity can be taken as a map of neoliberalism's irregular impact on the cost of property), middle-class dwellers can no longer hope for more than a mobile home. It is much easier to swallow this bitter pill if you can be assured (as Hart, Rhodes, and Morgan would like to do) that mobile home living is newly "respectable" and that its imitation of the physical and environmental characteristics of site built houses raises its status to a level consonant with financial stability and social security. Having the patina of security helps to compensate for the lowering of expectations: it also masks the fact that this newfound respectability is actually a clear symptom of the deterioration of the average American's quality of life. But how do mobile home residents reconcile themselves to this psychology? Is it adequate to their own assessment of the risks associated with their homes?

Because they tend to avoid nonempirical issues, Hart, Rhodes, and Morgan have little to say about residents' perceptions of risk. Halfway through their book, however, they mention a story in the *Minneapolis Star Tribune* that reported that a disproportionate percentage of police calls for domestic violence came from mobile home parks in the area. The story quoted a police supervisor in an uncommonly reveal-ing way: "You've got a different income level here, and some of the mentality is different. People of moderate income are more likely to call the police, while people with money try to hush it up. And the police are more likely to intervene in the lives of poor people" (85). While this comment tells us nothing conclusive about comparative levels of crime, it does give us a taste of the complexity of the circum-stances under which such data are collected. The kind of throwaway detail provided by the police source is all the more resonant because it is so rare in *The Unknown World of the Mobile Home*. What still remains unknown after reading this volume are the varieties of resi-dential psychology that only an ethnographer can expect to plumb. That is regrettable because our efforts to understand the mental and physical landscape of Beck's "risk society" could benefit just as much from field study of denizens of the trailer park (at least one doctoral thesis beckons!) as from Low's probing survey of the gated dweller. All the evidence suggests that we will need to know as much as we can about the *habitus* of insecurity as we enter yet another era of national political life governed by a state of full metal paranoia.

Even with Levitt's aforementioned comment in hand, it took a while for historians of the cold war to make some of the most telling links between mass suburbanization and the Truman Doctrine. Drawing on that lesson, we ought to be thinking right now about how the mili-tant shaping of the new unilateralism in U.S. foreign policy connects with the psychogeography of the nation. How pervasive among the citizenry is the obsession with security, and what can the study of land use tell us about its social and emotional mentality? How best to start building a relevant archive? Is it worth focusing even more closely on the rise of the Hummer lifestyle (to give a name to security-conscious consumerism) and on new permutations of home-owner association rules, or should we be looking at less obvious phenomena (trends in furnishing and decor, recreational patterns, obesity statistics, Home Depot marketing)? When placed in a broader research context, details like the advice on duct tape given by the Department of Homeland Security may turn out to yield some enduring significance rather than just go down in popular memory as one of the more ludicrous ideas thrown out by a desperate administration.

Whichever direction this research takes, residential ethnographies and landscape studies are two scholarly traditions that will prove to be particularly indispensable resources. The former needs to be revived and strengthened, especially in the area of suburbia, where it has fallen off in the past two decades; the agnostic legacy of the latter is all the more useful if we are to follow J. B. Jackson's example of eschewing moralism. Their insights should be consolidated with those from other disciplinary fields. More hard-hitting analyses of land development à la Mike Davis are required to lay bare the pathways of profit, and regional geographers will have to catch up with urbanists who see cities in the context of a globalizing economy. Critiques of form in design, architecture, and planning need to be integrated with the analysis of daily use pioneered in cultural studies. Then, and only then, will we have a fuller picture of what Davis calls the "ecology of fear" in a country that most of the world's population, when polled, appears to regard as the greatest threat to global stability.

2004

Notes

1. Edward James Blakely and Mary Gail Snyder, *Fortress America: Gated Communities in the United States* (Washington, DC: Brookings Institution Press, 1997).

2. Setha Low, *Behind the Gates: Life, Security, and the Pursuit of Happiness in Fortress America* (New York: Routledge, 2003); subsequent page references are given parenthetically in the text.

3. Ulrich Beck, *Risk Society: Towards a New Modernity* (Thousand Oaks, CA: Sage Publications, 1992).

4. Teresa Caldeira, *City of Walls: Crime, Segregation and Citizenship in São Paolo* (Berkeley: University of California Press, 2001).

5. John Fraser Hart, Michelle Rhodes, and John Morgan, *The Unknown World of the Mobile Home* (Baltimore: Johns Hopkins University Press, 2002), 1; subsequent page references are given parenthetically in the text.

11

Retro Urbanism: On the Once and Future TOD

Peter Hall

The point that worried Peter Calthorpe, over lunch last spring in Berkeley, is this: why does "New Urbanism" always seem to want to wear old clothes? Visit any of the archetypes—Poundbury, Kentlands, Celebration—and you are immediately borne back into the past. Poundbury is doubtless supposed to be reminiscent of nearby Dorset villages along that river quaintly called the Trent or Piddle, but even more uncannily it recalls a Lancashire mill town. Parts of Kentlands look like parts of Georgetown. Celebration resembles a streetcar suburb circa the turn of the past century.

This curious regression goes wider and deeper, of course. Look at any of the advertisements for the newest exurban developments from the Sunday *New York Times,* or from the London *Sunday Times,* and you will see the same old look. Commercial developments forty miles outside London, in the greenfields of Berkshire and Hampshire, are indistinguishable from my London suburb of Ealing, developed between 1880 and 1905, or from North Oxford, developed at about the same time. (When British TV wants a North Oxford house for its Inspector Morse series, it uses one in Ealing, much nearer and cheaper.) Similarly, developers in Connecticut and New Jersey seek to recapture the qualities of Brooklyn Heights or Forest Hills Gardens. Nostalgia sells.

Nostalgia sells for reasons hard and soft. It sells because old houses, or their imitations, offer good spaces—kids' bedrooms and playrooms, home offices, home gymnasiums—easily adaptable to different functions. But it sells also, and more importantly, because it offers symbolic virtues. Nostalgic architecture encapsulates a vision of a society that was, or seemed, more secure, grounded in fixed and shared values, a society in which people felt good about each other and treated one other decently. Such visions may, of course, be false. In any era, horrors of all sorts can lurk behind the picture windows; Sam Mendes's *American Beauty* is only the latest effort to pull back the curtains and expose what was intended to be hidden. The suburbia of 1900 may have been a hotbed of repression, child abuse, and other nastiness—made worse, perhaps, by the silence that then prevailed about such things. And, as we are reminded by the recent fascinating British television series *The 1900 House,* in which an entire family travels back one hundred years, middle-class life then depended upon backbreaking exertion on the part of servants and women; the sense of ease and spaciousness was made possible by someone endlessly stoking the furnace, laboriously cleaning clothes, preparing meals. But that is almost beside the point. What contemporary house buyers are seeking is not a real slice of life circa 1900 or so; they seek a fantasy, a sanitized version of reality, like the historical theme parks now found in every highly developed city in the world.

The point is that the suburb was always a place of escape from the city. That aspect was brilliantly captured in the deservedly famous late-nineteenth-century English railway suburb Bedford Park, described by Walter Creese as "the first sylvan setting for the middle class, where the nightingale and lark could still be heard."[1] John Lindley, who owned the land on which the suburb was built, was curator of the Royal Horticultural Society; his trees determined the ground plan; additional limes, poplars, and willows were planted. The result was noted at the time: the greenery broke up the hard lines of the houses, closing vistas and establishing space through filtered light. As John Betjeman put it, the paterfamilias could take pride in "A house of his own in the country."[2]

There is an uncanny parallel between Bedford Park and Forest Hills Gardens in the borough of Queens in New York City, begun some thirty-five years later. In the Queens development, too, the streets branch out from a commuter train station, with the shopping street on the other side. Forest Hills Gardens is famed as the place where the Russell Sage Foundation's resident sociologist, Clarence Perry,

Richard Norman Shaw, Bedford Park, Chiswick, England, 1875 onward. Photograph courtesy of Loeb Library at Harvard Graduate School of Design.

developed his concept of the neighborhood unit in the late 1920s. But Bedford Park, too, was a strong neighborhood, and while there is no indication in the planning history literature that Grosvenor Atterbury, the architect-planner of Forest Hills, consciously imitated Bedford Park, the similarities are so striking that it seems inconceivable he did not know of it.

Both Bedford Park and Forest Hills work brilliantly and are deservedly celebrated. But they work not because of their surface form but because of their function—both are deliberately and self-consciously *railway* suburbs. How right was one writer of the 1950s, recalling a Victorian childhood, who wrote, "Suburbia was a railway state . . . a state of existence within a few minutes walk of the railway station, a few minutes walk of the shops, and a few minutes walk of the fields."[3] Given that condition, all three—the railway, the shops, the open spaces—needed to be stressed as contributing to the success of any suburban design. These best of all suburbs are deliberately focused on a transit station and a cluster of shops and are at the same time so related to green space that they have a sense of semirural ease. The Victorian commuter, invariably male, left his rural retreat to walk to the station that would take him to the bustling city; he returned to an Arcadian retreat.[4] And, in the nineteenth-century gender division of labor, this retreat was occupied and managed throughout the day by women; it was a women's world.

That sense of separation was important because the late Victorian city was too often a decidedly unpleasant place: it was noisy (steel wheels on cobbled streets created an appalling din); it was smelly and dirty; it could be dangerous. Small wonder that when Raymond Unwin and Barry Parker came to create their own versions of the railway garden suburb, at Hampstead and Ealing in London in 1906 and 1907, they should have engaged in the conceit of trying to separate these places permanently from the evils of the city by a permanent greenbelt—at Hampstead, by an extension of Hampstead Heath; at Ealing, by a low river floodplain given over to playing fields and allotment gardens. Interestingly, though their urban design is wonderful at the level of the individual cluster of houses or even of entire streets, on the grander scale the conceit does not work well: the railway commuter is compelled to embark on an elongated walk through open space, charming perhaps on a summer evening, but less so on a chilly November night. Neither Hampstead nor Ealing has the physical or psychological coherence of Bedford Park or a dozen imitators that followed it, or of Forest Hills Gardens.

And the example of the best traditional suburbs underlines Peter Calthorpe's point. What the New Urbanism should be about, but in practice is seldom about, is recapturing not merely the form but also the functioning of the Victorian suburb. New Urbanism should be about what Calthorpe calls transit-oriented developments (TODs) or about what Robert Cervero and Michael Bernick have called transit villages: developments deliberately designed at densities higher than conventional automobile-oriented suburbs, that have shopping and other essential daily services within easy walking distance, and that are above all grouped around good transit.[5] On these clear and unequivocal criteria, few examples so far of the New Urbanism pass the test. Kentlands, a pure piece of auto-oriented suburbia some five miles beyond the end of the Washington, DC, Metro, certainly does not. Nor does Seaside, which is, after all, an isolated resort on the Florida coast.

And nor, unhappily, does Calthorpe's own ambitious venture, Laguna West, south of Sacramento. Calthorpe himself regards Laguna West as a failure and advised me not to go and see it; I ignored his advice and was glad I did, because the failure teaches important lessons.

The first failure, obvious within minutes of arrival, is that some-thing went drastically wrong with the design. The houses that follow Calthorpe's original concept, grouped tightly around a town hall and a manmade lake, are few; all around them are streets of banal tract houses designed on the most conventional lines around the demands of the automobile. What intervened were the failure of the original developer in the great Californian economic meltdown of the early 1990s and his replacement by a different developer sharing none of his predecessor's idealism or imagination.

But there is another and a deeper failure: in hardly any sense can this be called a *transit-oriented* development. The visitor or resident approaches Laguna West at seventy miles an hour via Interstate 5 and exits onto Laguna Boulevard, a monster six-lane arterial. On one side is a complex of low industrial buildings that might have been airlifted out of Silicon Valley (and indeed one of the biggest belongs to the Apple Computer Corporation). On the other side is a conventional shopping court development, and behind that a huge space waiting for something to happen.

What should be happening is the construction of the southern line of the Sacramento light-rail system, around which the entire develop-ment is, theoretically, oriented, and which is finally being built (and is scheduled to start operating in 2003). But the first and even the planned second stage will get nowhere near Laguna West; indeed it is heading in the wrong direction. Meanwhile, the commuter is offered a limited peak-hour express bus service on I-5, four buses each way on weekdays and nothing at any other time. In midafternoon the solitary bus shelter, unadorned by any information, looks almost derelict. The entire development feels as if it lacks a heart.

This, interestingly, underlines a central feature of Calthorpe's de-sign. At other places where he has done much smaller TODs—at Aggie Village in the campus town of Davis, near Sacramento, which is bus- and bike-based, and around a new train station at Mountain View in Silicon Valley—he has been compelled by physical and fiscal necessity to build closely and densely around transit and retail. But at Laguna West he was free to indulge in the creation of a grand vision. And what he did, in clear tribute to Ebenezer Howard, was to re-create the original 1898 diagram of the ideal Garden City.

To be specific, to accommodate the transit station—an element inci-dental to Howard, who was designing not a suburb but a self-contained settlement—Calthorpe had to chop Howard's circular central space in half. But otherwise it is all there just as Howard saw it: a vast formal central space, with processional avenues radiating out over the lake and through parks and playing fields, and with key public buildings like a town hall, a day center for children, and a school. And beyond that, just as Howard conceived them, were the residential districts. That this should have been built in 1992 is all the more astonishing, because neither Letchworth nor Welwyn, as built, turned out like that; seeing Laguna West is like seeing *Garden Cities of Tomorrow* in a dream that has become astonishingly real.

Laguna West could have been brilliant. The few original houses, designed in a fresh idiom that subtly evokes century-old California streetcar suburbs, show the urban qualities that might have been achieved. And when—and if—the transit ever arrives, Calthorpe's idealistic vision might still be realized. But it is fatally compromised by the rest of the development, which exhibits every perverse design feature against which the New Urbanists have railed: houses that turn their backs to streets, so that the motorist sees nothing but fences; overly wide streets with no urbanity; huge detached houses that have no relation to the streetscape or landscape or anything at all in the vicinity. It is an opportunity tragically missed. And more than that: precisely because it is all so completely automobile dependent, in a part of California that is traditionally auto dependent anyway, it makes more dubious the economics of extending the light-rail.

Calthorpe is now designing some big new schemes, above all on the site of the old Stapleton Airport at Denver, which may at last allow him to realize a true New Urbanist place. But at present, apart from a handful of mini-schemes by Calthorpe and others—such as an interesting apartment development next to the El Cerrito del Norte station of the San Francisco BART—the sad fact is that there are no true examples of the New Urbanism, rigorously defined as such, in America today.

And neither, it might be argued, are any to be found in England. Poundbury, for all its architectural qualities, is essentially a housing scheme on the edge of a small English town, next to the bypass road. It is as car dependent as any such development is bound to be, and this is exacerbated by the fact that the town center shops show serious signs of decay, and the nearest major retail and employment centers are twenty or more miles away. The new Millennium Village at Greenwich near London, next to Richard Rogers's Millennium Dome, which began construction this spring, could do better: it is on an electronically guided busway connecting it in a few minutes to a subway station. But the busway is not yet complete and seems to be dogged by problems; the nearest retail is a large superstore, labeled "low-energy" but not within easy walking distance for many of the residents. Opposite it on the other side of the Thames at Silvertown, another self-styled "urban village" lacks both employment and adequate shops; it will get light-rail transit around 2003, about when it is completed.

At least these last two developments will have some of the key elements that most planners, echoing Calthorpe, would deem essential for transit-oriented development. Most basic of all will be adequate transit service. Further, both are clearly and unambiguously brownfield regeneration schemes in a part of the city enjoying massive renewal. What is yet unclear, either in the United States or in England, is whether planners can achieve what their Swedish counterparts achieved around Stockholm half a century ago: new greenfield developments structured around high-quality transit service and with retail and other key services right outside the transit stations, within easy walking access for all. It was done there, and it could be done elsewhere, as Colin Ward and I have suggested in our book *Sociable Cities*. We could build small garden cities, very much like country towns, around commuter train or light-rail or bus stops. We know how to do it. We did it in those classic railroad suburbs a century ago, which people still love so much that they are prepared to pay a lot of money to live in them. And planners like Calthorpe have shown that we can do it here and now, if only we can coordinate transit planning with new residential development, and if only we can find developers with the necessary courage and vision.

But will we? The answer is not clear. For the problem does not seem to be that developers are boneheadedly conservative and unimaginative, unresponsive to home buyers clamoring for something better. Calthorpe's smaller schemes—at Mountain View and at Aggie Village—have proved marketable enough. But they sell mostly to a niche market—to buyers with imagination and education—while most Americans seem willing to stick with the familiar and the bland. But real *New* Urbanism—as distinct from its cosmetic version—demands expensive upfront investment in transit schemes; otherwise residents will take to their cars, and the battle to change suburbia will be lost from the start. This suggests that successful new urbanism must be conceived on a large scale, accompanied by a major public commitment. California, despite brave intentions, has not quite brought it off. Maybe Denver, or Salt Lake City where Calthorpe has recently been working, will do better. Anyone who really cares about alternatives to the auto-dependent suburb should watch these places closely.

2000

Notes

1. Walter L. Creese, *The Search for Environment: The Garden City Before and After* (New Haven: Yale University Press, 1966), 89.

2. Quoted in Creese, *The Search for Environment,* 91–92.

3. James Kenward, *The Suburban Child* (Cambridge: Cambridge University Press, 1955), 74.

4. Peter Hall, "East Thames Corridor: The Second Golden Age of the Garden Suburb" (The Kevin Lynch Memorial Lecture, 1991/2), *Urban Design Quarterly* 43, 1992: 6

5. Peter Calthorpe, *The Next American Metropolis: Ecology, Community, and the American Dream* (New York: Princeton Architectural Press, 1993); Michael Bernick and Robert Cervero, *Transit Villages in the 21st Century* (New York: McGraw Hill, 1997).

Contributors

Mike Davis, a MacArthur fellow, is the author of *City of Quartz, Ecology of Fear, Magical Urbanism: Latinos Reinvent the U.S. Big City,* and other books.

Ellen Dunham-Jones is associate professor and director of the architecture program at Georgia Institute of Technology.

Robert Fishman teaches at the Taubman College of Architecture and Planning at the University of Michigan, Ann Arbor. He is the author of *Bourgeois Utopias: The Rise and Fall of Suburbia.*

Sir Peter Hall is professor of planning at University College London. His most recent books are *Urban and Regional Planning* and *Urban 21: A Global Agenda for Twenty-first Century Cities.*

David Harvey is distinguished professor at the City College of New York Graduate Center. His books include *The Condition of Postmodernity, The New Imperialism,* and *Paris, Capital of Modernity.*

Jerold S. Kayden, a lawyer and city planner, is the Frank Backus Williams Professor of Urban Planning and Design at Harvard University Graduate

School of Design. He is author of *Privately Owned Public Space: The New York City Experience,* coauthor of *Landmark Justice,* and coeditor of *Zoning and the American Dream.*

Matthew J. Kiefer is a partner at the Boston-based law firm of Goulston & Storrs, where he practices real estate development and land-use law, with a focus on obtaining site control and public approvals for complex urban projects. He is also lecturer in urban planning at Harvard University Graduate School of Design.

Alex Krieger is professor of urban design at Harvard Design School and a partner at Chan Krieger & Associates, Cambridge. He is author of *Past Futures: Two Centuries of Imagining Boston* and editor of *Mapping Boston.*

Andrew Ross is professor of American studies at New York University and author of several books, including *Anti-Americanism; Low Pay, High Profile: The Global Push for Fair Labor; No-Collar: The Humane Workplace and Its Hidden Costs;* and *The Celebration Chronicles.*

James S. Russell is editor-at-large for *Architectural Record* and also writes for *Wall Street Journal,* the *New York Times,* the *Philadelphia Inquirer,* and *Business Week.* He teaches urban design at Columbia University.

William S. Saunders is editor of *Harvard Design Magazine.* He is the author of *Modern Architecture: Photographs of Ezra Stoller.*

Mitchell Schwarzer is professor of architecture, art history, and visual studies at the California College of Arts and Crafts, and chair of the school's Program in Visual Studies. He is author of *Zoomscape: Architecture in Motion and Media* and *German Architectural Theory and the Search for Modern Identity.*